W0248339

NEW

Step in

ANGLAIS

LANGUE VIVANTE 1

3e

Marie-Aude Ligozat
Direction pédagogique

Odile Bontout
Collège du Pont du Bois, Saint-Chéron

Danièle Broussaud
Collège Joseph Bara, Palaiseau

Aliki Diaz-Kostakis
École Polytechnique, Palaiseau

Maryse Pelletier
Collège Martin Luther King, Buc

HATIER

Création :
Graphismes

Réalisation :
Graphismes

Illustrations des *Units* :
Dominique Fages

Illustrations de *Story time* :
François San Millan (pp. 118–127)
et
Yves Besnier (pp. 116-117)

Cartographie :
Corédoc, Laurent Blondel

Préface

Les sept unités de ***New Step in 3e*** vont vous permettre de voyager dans le monde anglophone et de découvrir certains aspects de sa culture, tout en renforçant votre maîtrise de la langue.

Vous aimez voyager…

Les deux **pages d'ouverture** vous donnent les informations essentielles sur l'histoire et la géographie du pays et la rubrique ***More about …*** vous fournit des renseignements complémentaires sur les habitants du pays, le mode de vie, les attraits touristiques …

Vous vous intéressez à la musique, au cinéma…

Deux unités vous offrent un panorama de la musique anglo-saxonne et du cinéma américain.

Vous souhaitez développer vos connaissances en anglais …

- Les trois ***Basics*** vous permettent de pratiquer les structures syntaxiques de la langue tout en découvrant de nouveaux aspects du pays ou du thème concerné.
- Les courts dialogues des ***Listening*** mettant en scène des jeunes de votre âge vous entraînent à la compréhension orale de l'anglais, qu'il soit parlé par des Américains, des Australiens, des Irlandais… ou des Anglais !
- La rubrique ***Topic*** vous donne accès à des textes variés à propos desquels vous serez amenés à échanger des points de vue avec vos camarades de classe et à exprimer vos opinions personnelles. Comme en 4e vous aurez l'occasion de prendre la parole en continu, et des exercices guidés vous aideront à améliorer votre expression écrite.
- La rubrique ***More words*** vous permet d'enrichir votre vocabulaire.

Vous cherchez de l'aide dans votre manuel…

- La rubrique ***Remember and Practise*** vous explique les phénomènes de la langue et vous offre différents exercices de renforcement.
- Le ***Mémento grammatical*** reprend l'ensemble des connaissances grammaticales exigibles en collège.
- La partie ***Outils méthodologiques*** vous initie au commentaire d'un document visuel, à la rédaction d'une lettre et au maniement du dictionnaire.
- Le ***Lexique*** à double entrée (anglais - français / français - anglais) vous permet de trouver rapidement le mot que vous recherchez.

Vous voulez lire pour le plaisir…

Vous vous reportez aux pages ***Story Time*** de votre manuel. Dans la diversité des textes proposés, vous trouverez de quoi satisfaire vos goûts de lecteur avisé … ou débutant !

Bon courage et très bonne année scolaire !

Les auteurs.

Structure d'une unité

Ouverture de l'unité

- Elle présente les informations essentielles sur la géographie, l'histoire et la culture du pays ou du thème abordé dans l'unité.
- Un quiz dans le *workbook* réactive les informations présentées sur ces pages.

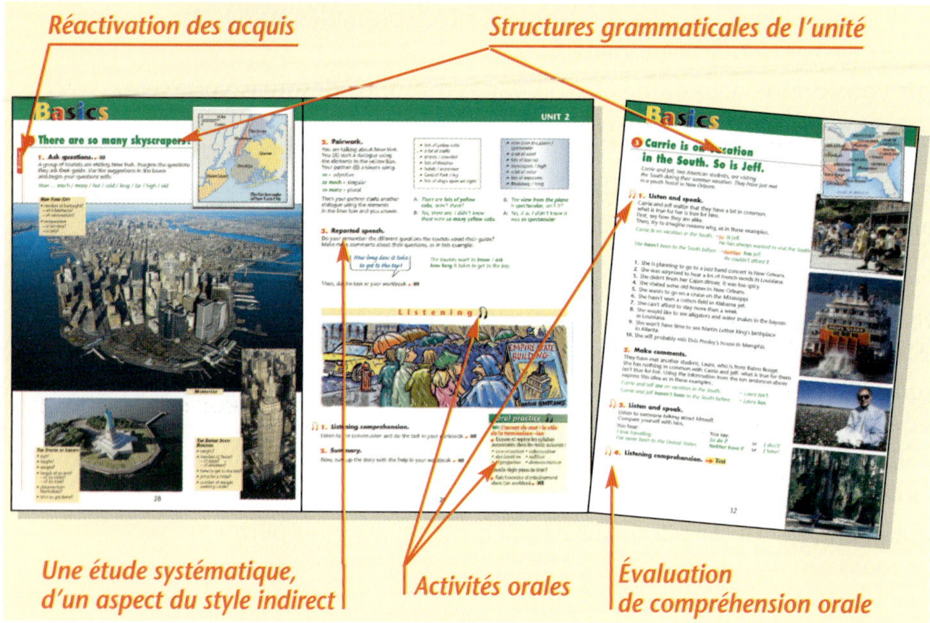

Basics

- Les pages *Basics* réactivent des points de langue (*Review*) et introduisent les structures grammaticales au programme de 3e sous forme d'activités communicatives.
- Ces structures sont développées dans le *workbook* par la Pratique Raisonnée de la Langue.

More words

- Une vingtaine de mots enregistrés et accompagnés d'activités orales. Ce lexique enrichit le vocabulaire et prépare au texte du *Topic*.
- Des activités écrites sont proposées dans le *workbook*.

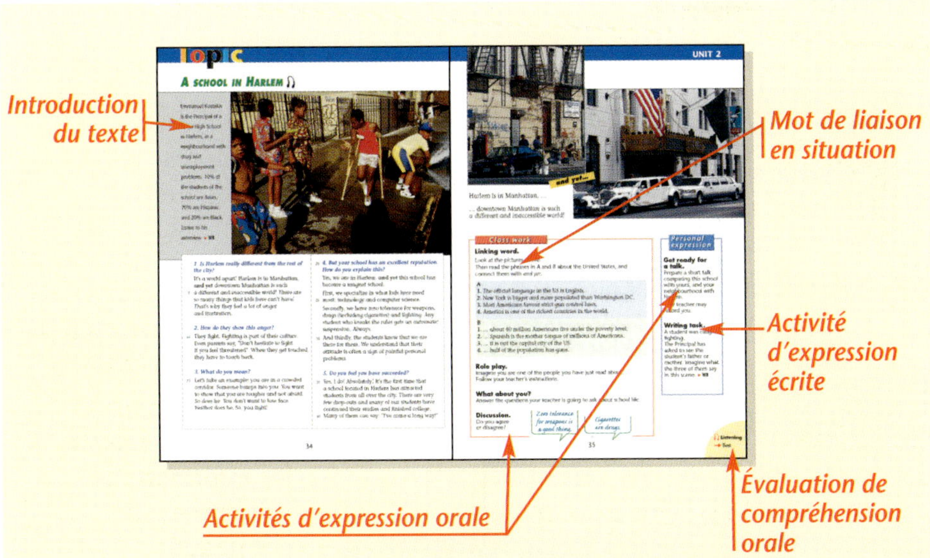

Topic

- Des textes courts qui réactivent les structures des ***Basics*** et qui favorisent diverses formes d'expression orale ou écrite guidée.

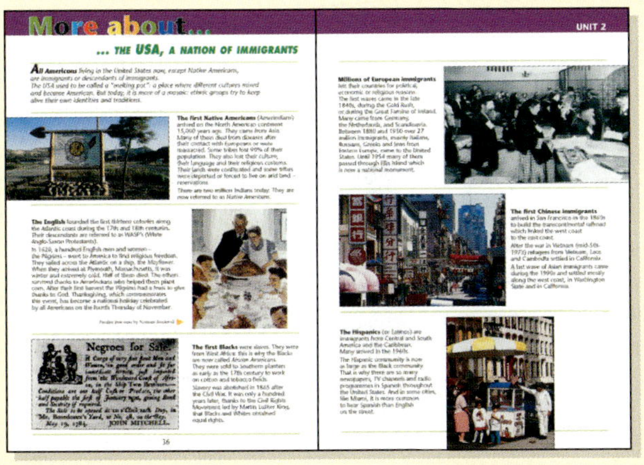

More about…

- Des informations complémentaires sur le pays, les hommes, leur histoire et leur mode de vie…

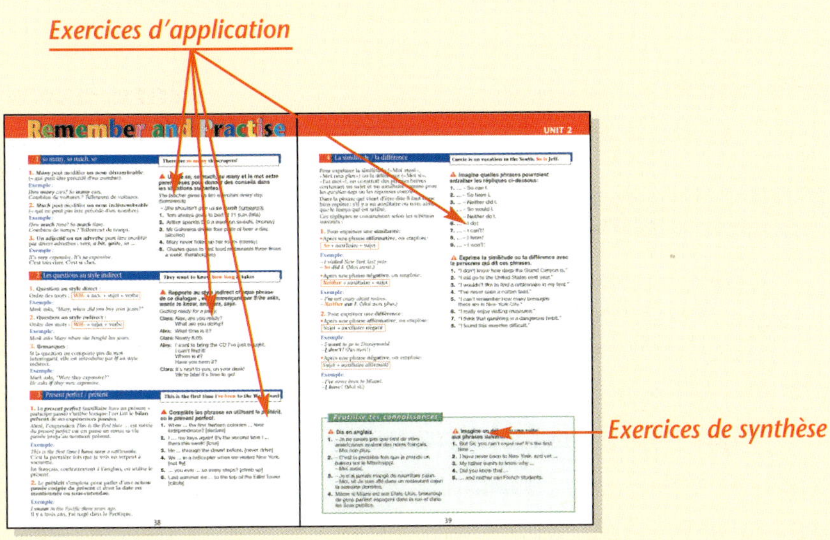

Remember and Practise

- Récapitulatif des structures grammaticales étudiées dans l'unité avec des exercices de renforcement.

Sommaire

Objectifs fonctionnels et grammaticaux	Objectifs phonologiques
■ le prétérit simple (***Review***); la similitude : *both of us / neither of us* ■ prétérit simple / prétérit *be* + *-ing* (***Review***) ■ le style indirect : changement de référents (***Review***) ■ la réciprocité : *each other* ■ la formation des mots : le suffixe *-ly* ■ l'expression du contraste : *whereas*	■ la terminaison *-ic* ■ liaisons, formes faibles, mots accentués et inaccentués
■ les questions en *How* (***Review***) ; expression d'une quantité : *so, so much, so many* ■ le style indirect : les questions au style indirect ■ *le present perfect* : *They have been to* (***Review***) ; *It's the first time …* ■ la similitude et la différence : *so / neither did I; I did / I didn't* ■ la formation des mots : les préfixes *un-; ir-; im-, in-* ■ l'expression de la concession : *and yet*	■ la terminaison *-ion* ■ l'accentuation des pronoms personnels
■ les pronoms relatifs (***Review***) et le relatif *when* ■ exprimer la contrainte et la permission : *let / make someone do* ■ le style indirect avec *say / tell* ■ parler de ce qui était vrai autrefois et qui ne l'est plus : *used to; not … any more* ■ la formation des mots : les suffixes *-ful et -less* ■ l'expression du but : *so that*	■ la terminaison *-ian* ■ les consonnes qui disparaissent à l'oral
■ la voix passive (***Review***) ■ le style indirect : le passage du présent au prétérit ■ la voix passive avec les verbes *ask, give, tell, offer, show …* ■ les verbes *look / sound* + adj. ■ le gérondif après les prépositions ■ les verbes *look / sound like*+ noms ■ la formation des mots : le suffixe *-ness* ■ l'expression du résultat : *As a result*	■ les terminaisons *-er / -or* ■ la forme en *-ing* / la forme passive en *-en*

UNIT 5 — Welcome to the United Kingdom!

UNIT 6 — Australia, a country and a continent

UNIT 7 — Visit Ireland, the Emerald Isle

Objectifs fonctionnels et grammaticaux	Objectifs phonologiques
■ le conditionnel : *I'd like / ...* (***Review***); *if* + prétérit, ... *would* + base verbale ■ le style indirect : *wonder* ■ l'expression de la préférence : *I'd rather ... than ...* ■ les composés en *WH-ever* ■ la formation des mots : les mots composés (*a fashion designer, ...)* ■ l'expression de la restriction : *as long as*	■ les premières syllabes *a-* ou *be-* ■ l'accent secondaire

■ le comparatif (***Review***); le double comparatif ■ le style indirect: le passage de *will* à *would* ■ faire le bilan d'une activité récente: le *present perfect* avec *be + -ing* ■ *for / since ...* (***Review***); *le present perfect* avec *be + -ing ... for / since ...* ■ la formation des mots: les mots composés (*a driving licence, ...)* ■ l'expression de la concession: *even though*	■ les terminaisons en voyelles doubles ou en *–ese* ■ la forme d'insistance : les auxiliaires accentués

■ exprimer l'antériorité: *le past perfect* ■ le style indirect: le passage du *present perfect* au *past perfect* ■ le conditionnel: *If + past perfect, ... would have* + participe passé ■ l'expression du regret: *I wish + prétérit; I wish + past perfect* ■ la formation des mots: les mots composés (*open-minded, ...)* ■ l'expression de la restriction: *unless*	■ la terminaison *-ity* ■ les prononciations de *have*

PLEASED TO MEET YOU!

You

- I was born on … (*day*) in … (*year*)
- I look like …
- I'm a bit … / extremely … / I'm not … at all.
- I am an "early bird" / a late riser / a "night owl".

Your tastes and hobbies

- I'm crazy about …
- I enjoy … / I don't really like …
- I practise … / I play … / I collect …

Your relationships with people

- I like people who …
- I can't stand people who …
- I get on well with …
- I've known my best friend for … / since …

Your personal experiences

- I've been to … / I have never been to …
- I have never …
- The nicest person I know is …

At the seaside
[sailing, windsurfing, waterskiing, fishing, snorkelling, …]

In the mountains
[rock-climbing, rafting, kayaking, …]

In the country
[hiking, fishing, horse-riding, poney-trekking, …]

Your last summer holidays

- I went / didn't go abroad / to …
- I stayed at …
- I spent … in … with …
- I went hiking / horse-riding …

Your school life

- My second foreign language is …
- I have / haven't taken an optional subject (technology / Latin / Greek ...)
- My favourite subject is …
- I'm better at ... than at ...
- I'm not good at …
- I walk / cycle to school / I go to school by …

Your future job

- I'd like / I wouldn't like to be a ... because ...
- My parents would like me to …
- I've already seen the careers advisor. / I haven't seen (her / him) yet.

1. Speak.

Complete some of the sentences above to introduce yourself as in this example:

I'm better at maths than at French.

2. Pairwork.

Ask your partners:

1. when and where they were born;
2. if they play a musical instrument;
3. where they spent their last summer holidays;
4. if they have ever been abroad. If so, where;
5. if they will look for a job as soon as they leave school.

Then introduce your partners to the rest of the class, as in this example:

Sarah has been to Rome.

1 The sounds of music

Objectifs

1— Le prétérit simple
When did both of them become famous?

2— Prétérit simple / prétérit *be + -ing*
What was going on? What happened?
Le style indirect : changement de référents

3— La réciprocité
They looked at each other.

How much do you know about music?

QUIZ

Look at the documents, then do the quiz in your workbook. ▸ **WB, p. 4**

WORK SONGS

The times of slavery

On big plantations in the South of the United States, Black slaves sang *work songs* while they were picking cotton or cutting sugar cane. Slaves had to use English and were not allowed to sing in their native languages or use traditional African instruments such as drums.
These songs are the roots of much of the music we listen to today.

THE BLUES AND GOSPEL

From the 1860s on

The *blues* was born in the Southern States of the USA after the abolition of slavery (1861). It expressed the feelings of Black people in their everyday lives: their hopes, their loneliness, their day-to-day troubles.

Negro spirituals and *gospel* are religious songs based on the Bible, expressing hope and revolt.

JAZZ

From the early 1900s

The first *jazz* bands appeared in New Orleans, Louisiana. The musicians were black. They played cheap instruments like the guitar, the banjo, the trumpet, or even the washboard.
Jazz musicians include world-famous artists like the singer and trumpet player Louis Armstrong (1900-1971), the pianist Duke Ellington (1899-1974), and the saxophone player Charlie Parker (1920-1955).

ROCK'N'ROLL

The 50s

Rhythm'n'blues–a combination of jazz and blues–became popular among Black American singers. One of the most famous groups was the Platters.

Then Black singers transformed rhythm'n'blues into a new kind of music: *rock'n'roll*.
But the *King* of rock'n'roll was Elvis Presley, a white Southerner who sang like a black man.

FROM ROCK TO RAP

The 1960s and 1970s

Rock'n'roll evolved and became *rock* which includes many kinds of music from *pop music* (with the very successful British groups *The Beatles* and *The Rolling Stones*) to *hip-hop* (the sound of America's streets).

The 1990s

Rap artists continue the African storytelling tradition and speak about racial, social and economic problems.

❶ When did both of them become famous?

Review

1. Ask questions. ▸ WB, pp. 6-7

Ask your teacher questions to know more about Elvis Presley, using the verbs around the picture.

2. Group work.

The class is divided into two groups.
Group A has information about Bob Marley, and group B about John Lennon.
Each group asks questions to fill in the grids in the workbook. ▸ WB, p. 7

3. Make comments. ▶ WB, p. 8

Use the information from your grids and say what John Lennon and Bob Marley had in common, as in this example:

***Both of them** gave concerts all over the world.*

4. What about you?

You are going to work with a partner to find out what you have in common.

Ask questions to know:
- which singers or groups both of you like or don't like;
- if you ever listen to classical music;
- if you play a musical instrument;
- if you have ever been to a concert;
- if you have ever been to the opera;
- if you enjoy dancing.

Now, tell the class how you and your partner are alike, as in these examples:
***Both of us** listen to classical music. / **Neither of us** listens to classical music.*

Listening

1. Listening comprehension.

Listen to the conversation and do the task in your workbook.
▶ WB, pp. 8-9

2. Summary.

Now, sum up the story with the help in your workbook. ▶ WB, p. 9

Oral practice

L'accent de mot : le rôle de la terminaison *-ic*

■ Ecoute et repère les syllabes accentuées dans les mots suivants :
- *music*
- *lyrics*
- *artistic*
- *fantastic*
- *enthusiastic*

Quelle règle peux-tu tirer ?

■ Fais l'exercice d'entraînement dans ton *workbook*. ▶ WB, p. 8

2 What was going on? What happened?

1. What was going on? ▸ WB, p. 10

Look at the pictures **A** and **B** and say what was going on at the same time on stage and in the audience, using the verbs and expressions in the box, as in this example:

__While__ the band __was__ play__ing__, people in the audience __were__ danc__ing__.

- *dance*
- *scream*
- *clap their hands*
- *sing along with the music*
- *film*
- *record the concert*
- *hold hands*
- *take pictures*

2. What happened? ▶ WB, p. 11

Now, look at the drawings 1 to 7 .
Using the verbs in the box, say what happened during the concert, as in this example:

***While** the band **was** play**ing**, a girl climb**ed** onto the stage.*

- *climb*
- *rip off*
- *(the spotlights) go out*
- *faint*
- *take ... hand*
- *(the amplifiers) break down*
- *fall in love*

3. Listen.

Listen to the recording and choose the right answer. ▶ WB, p. 12

4. Reported speech. ▶ WB, p. 12

Look at the drawings on page 16 and report what Kate, Tom, Ted and Lucy say, as in this example:

Ted says: *I love you!*

*He says that **he** loves **her**.*

Listening

1. Listening comprehension.

Listen to the conversation and do the task in your workbook. ▶ WB, p. 13

2. Summary.

Now, sum up the story with the help in your workbook. ▶ WB, p. 13

Oral practice

Liaisons, formes faibles, mots accentués et inaccentués

■ Tu as appris dans *New Step in 4ème* que pour se faire comprendre à l'oral ou pour comprendre l'oral, plusieurs phénomènes sont à prendre en considération.
Ecoute et repère dans les exemples ci-dessous :

- les liaisons :
  All of a sudden the lights went out.
  He fell in love with her.
- les formes faibles :
  He was listening to the music.
  Ted and Lucy were dancing.
- les mots accentués :
  While the band was playing, people in the audience were dancing.
  While the band was playing, a girl climbed onto the stage.

■ Fais l'exercice d'entraînement dans ton *workbook*. ▶ WB, p. 12

3 They looked at each other.

1. The beginning of a love story. ▸ WB, p. 14

Tell the beginning of this love story, using *each other* or *themselves* with the verbs given, as in these examples.

*They looked at **each other**.*

*They said to **themselves**, "Wow!!"*

[smile at ...]

[say hello to ...]

[introduce ... to ...]

[talk to ...]

[ask ... if ...]

[ask ... for ...]

[think about ...]

[send messages to ...]

[see ... often]

2. How did this love story end?

Imagine two different endings to the story: a happy one and a sad one. Use the verbs in the box and *each other*.

- *get on with ...*
- *get bored with ...*
- *love ... forever*
- *end up hating ...*
- *never leave ...*
- *never see ... again*
- *start to argue with ...*

3. Listening comprehension. → Test

More Words

MUSIC AND MUSICIANS ▸ WB, p. 15

musician	*musicien*
pop music	*musique de variétés*
performer	*artiste (de scène)*
composer	*compositeur*
band	*groupe de musique*
orchestra ['ɔːkɪstrə]	*orchestre classique*
conductor [kən'dʌktə]	*chef d'orchestre*
tune [tjuːn]	*air de musique*
lyrics	*paroles*
chorus ['kɔːrəs]	*refrain*
record [rɪ'kɔːd]	*enregistrer*
record ['rekəd]/['rekɔːd]	*disque*
recording	*enregistrement*
rehearse [rɪ'hɜːs]	*répéter*
rehearsal [rɪ'hɜːsl]	*répétition*
sound [saʊnd]	*son*
rhythm / beat ['rɪðm] [biːt]	*rythme*
drums	*batterie*
drummer	*batteur*
keyboard	*clavier*
violin [vaɪə'lɪn]	*violon*
earphones	*écouteurs*
mike [maɪk]	*micro*
play (the ...)	*jouer de (...)*
low [ləʊ]	*bas*
loud [laʊd]	*fort*
copy ['kɒpɪ]	*exemplaire (disque, journal, livre)*

1. Listen and repeat.
Listen and repeat the words from the list.

2. Listen and answer.
Listen to the questions
and give the right answer.

3. A hidden message.

ðeə sɒŋz mɪkst ðə 'rɪðm əv
dʒæz ən bluːz

Coin New Words

Most adverbs are created by adding the suffix *–ly* to an adjective.
Look at the following examples:

particular → particularly **real → really** **easy → easily**

Now, do the exercise in your workbook. ▸ WB, p. 15

BECOMING A POP STAR

Several TV programmes today try to discover new talents among young people and make pop stars out of them. Each week the viewers vote to eject one of the candidates and the finalist – a group or a solo artist – goes on tour and records an album. David, 20, participated in one of these programmes. ▸ **WB, pp. 16-17**

1. David, did you have any singing experience before this?

No, unfortunately, I didn't. All of the others had some musical training, **whereas** I didn't have any at all, and I felt I was a bit behind. That's why I stayed on the programme for only three weeks.

2. What was the training like?

Hard! Everyday was a packed day–from 6 a.m. to 11 p.m.!–with dance classes, vocal classes, and strict workout sessions. A star has to be–and stay–fit because you need a lot of energy to get through rehearsals and the live Friday shows.

3. How did you feel when you were eliminated?

While I was waiting for the results of the votes my heart was pounding, I was trembling and sweating. And when I heard my name, I was disappointed but I was expecting it: I knew that girls supported me, **whereas** most boys didn't.

4. What were the toughest moments?

Well, as time went on, we got irritated by each other, and then the group began to crack and jealousies came out. And also sometimes I felt very homesick. I missed my family and my girlfriend very much.

5. Do you regret this experience?

Oh, not at all! It was thrilling! Today I'm fitter, I'm a better dancer and a better singer–thanks to the terrific teachers–and I have more confidence in myself. I also realized that talent isn't enough to be a star. You have to be prepared to work very, very hard. And most of all, you absolutely must have a strong will to win.

I knew that girls supported me, ... *most boys didn't.*

Class work

Linking word. ▶ WB, p. 17

Read the caption under the two pictures above.
Then read the phrases in A and B about those TV shows, and connect them with *whereas*.

A

1. Most singers usually have very little dancing experience,
2. Certain candidates who sing very well are eliminated,
3. For some contestants it's easy to adapt to life in a group,
4. Most singers have to work for many years before they become popular,

B

1. ... "pop stars" become famous in a few months.
2. ... "pop stars" benefit from intensive dancing training.
3. ... candidates who aren't as good become finalists.
4. ... it can be a nerve-racking experience for others.

Role play.

Imagine you are one of the people you have just read about. Follow your teacher's instructions.

What about you?

Answer the questions your teacher is going to ask about what role music plays in your life.

Discussion.

Do you agree or disagree?

A star has to be – and stay – fit.

Talent isn't enough to be a star.

Personal expression

Get ready for a talk.

Try to convince the producers of a TV programme that you have the qualities of a pop star.

Your teacher may record you.

Writing task.

Your favourite contestant was eliminated. You think that it was unfair and you write a letter to protest. ▶ WB, p. 18

Listening → Test

More about...

... SONGS ROOTED IN REBELLION. ▸ WB, p. 19

The "protest songs" of the sixties were above all anti-war songs, criticizing the American intervention in Vietnam.
These songs–and the popular slogan of the times ("Peace and Love")–reflected the hope for a better future. They also became associated with the struggle against racial segregation and for civil rights.

The Woodstock Festival in 1969 became a symbol of the hippie movement, a movement which rejected the traditional American way of life. Nearly half a million people came and for three consecutive days, they listened to famous musicians or singers like the guitarist Jimi Hendrix.

Reggae was born in the late 60s in the poor districts of Kingston, Jamaica. It combined the slow dance rhythms of Jamaican music and the strong beat of rhythm'n'blues and ska.
The lyrics have both a political and a philosophical message encouraging Black people to "stand up and fight for [their] rights". They express the ideas of Rastafarianism–a Jamaican spiritual movement. It is based on the belief in "Jah" (God) and in Africa–especially Ethiopia–as the promised land for Black people.

Bob Marley introduced reggae to the world in the mid-seventies. He became a national hero and a world-famous star.

In the mid-seventies the British group *Sex Pistols* shocked British society with their subversive **punk music**. They were reacting against electronic music played on commercial radios and against rock groups they considered boring and conventional. They were also rebelling against a conservative society suffering from unemployment and social problems.

In 1977, while Britain was celebrating the Queen's Silver Jubilee, the *Sex Pistols* sang their unpatriotic song:

God save the Queen
She ain't no human being
There's no future in England's dreaming.

It was banned by radio stations but became number one on the charts.

"No future" became the slogan of young people who expressed their frustration and anger through this music but also through the way they dressed.

In the eighties, **rap music** first appeared in the Bronx, a poor Hispanic and Black neighbourhood in New York City. Later, many Black rappers like the group *Public Enemy* became popular throughout the United States and Europe.

Rap songs tell stories about the conditions of ghetto life and express frustration, anger and disgust. Rappers sometimes try to shock audiences and the lyrics of their songs can be extremely violent, racist or homophobic, with crude language and attacks against women or the police.

The rap artist Eminem became famous in the early 2000s: he showed that a white singer could also express himself through rap.

Remember and Practise

1 Le prétérit simple

1. Rappel de la formation du prétérit simple :

• **Forme affirmative :**
La marque du temps est sur le verbe, que celui-ci soit régulier (*They compose**d***) ou irrégulier (*They **wrote***).

• **Formes interrogative et négative :**
La marque du temps n'est plus sur le verbe, mais sur l'auxiliaire ***did***.

Exemples :

***Did** they compose ... ?*	***Did** they write ... ?*
*They **didn't** compose ...*	*They **didn't** write ...*

• **Remarque :**
Attention à la forme du prétérit de *be*, qui, étant à la fois un verbe et un auxiliaire, ne s'emploie jamais avec l'auxiliaire *did*.

Exemples :

*They **weren't** British. **Were** they American?*

2. Emploi du prétérit simple:

Le prétérit s'utilise pour raconter **un fait** qui est **terminé** et qui est **sans lien avec le moment où l'on parle**. C'est pourquoi ce temps est utilisé – entre autres – dans un récit ou une biographie.

When did both of them become famous?

⚠ Réfère-toi à la frise chronologique page 13 et écris les questions qui amènent les réponses suivantes:

1. Work songs.
2. After the abolition of slavery.
3. In New Orleans, Louisiana.
4. The guitar, the banjo, the trumpet, and even the washboard.
5. In the 1970s.

⚠ Corrige ces affirmations qui sont toutes inexactes, comme dans l'exemple suivant:

Elvis Presley died in 1950.
→ *No, he didn't die in 1950! He died in 1977.*

1. Elvis Presley became famous during WWII. He was born in New York.
2. John Lennon had many children. He started singing at the age of 20.
3. Bob Marley was American. He sang rap music.

2 Prétérit simple / prétérit *be + -ing*

On peut adopter des points de vue (aspects) différents pour évoquer des faits passés.

• Lorsque l'on veut donner un « **coup de projecteur** » sur la situation ou l'activité dans laquelle on se trouvait **à un moment du passé**, on utilise la forme:

was / were + -ing

Exemple :

*What **were** you do**ing** yesterday at 5.30?*
Que faisais-tu hier à 17h30?

• Lorsqu'il y a ***plusieurs activités simultanées***, pour tous les verbes on utilise la même forme:

was / were + -ing

Exemple :

***While** the musicians **were** play**ing**, everybody **was** danc**ing**.*
Pendant que les musiciens jouaient, tout le monde dansait.

• Lorsqu'**une activité en cours est interrompue par un événement** ou une succession d'événements, on utilise le **prétérit *be + -ing*** (activité en cours) et un **prétérit simple** (événement).

Exemple :

*While the guitarist **was** play**ing**, the amplifiers **broke down**.*
Pendant que le guitariste jouait *(activité en cours)*, les amplificateurs ont sauté *(événement)*.

What was going on? What happened?

▲ Mets les verbes entre crochets au prétérit simple ou au prétérit en *be + -ing* selon le cas.

1. Yesterday I [study] in my room, when my brother [put] his radio on at full blast. I [get] mad at him!
2. Mum was furious too, because she [listen] to music and she couldn't hear it.
3. So, she [go] to Tom's room and [bang] on the door.
4. Tom [not answer], so she [go] into his room.
5. You know what? Tom [lie] quietly on his bed, he [sing] along with the music, his eyes closed, and he [smile].

3 Le style indirect : changement de référents

He says he loves her.

• Lorsque l'on rapporte les paroles de quelqu'un, il se peut qu'il n'y ait aucune modification des paroles prononcées.

Exemple :

*Mike: "**The concert is going to start.**"*
*→ He says that **the concert is going to start**.*

• Mais lorsque l'on rapporte des paroles dont le référent (= la personne dont on parle) est **à la première ou à la deuxième personne** (*I / me / my; we / us / our; you / your*), il y a un **changement de référent**.

Exemples :

*Ted (to Lucy): "**I** love **you**."*
*→ He says that **he** loves **her**.*

*Lucy (to Ted): "**I** love **you**."*
*→ She says that **she** loves **him**.*

*Mary's parents : "**We**'ll take **our** car."*
*→ They say that **they**'ll take **their** car.*

▲ Rapporte chacune des phrases ci-dessous au style indirect.

1. Emma: "I have never been to a classical music concert, but my parents have."
2. Dave: "When I do my homework, I put my radio on."
3. Chris and Harry: "We often sing during our music lessons."
4. Kate (to Zoe): "I'll lend you my CD if you want to copy it."
5. Emily: "I play the violin, but I can't play it at school, because we don't have a school orchestra."
6. Tony: "When I listen to rap, I feel good. It's like someone talking directly to me."

4 La réciprocité

They looked at each other.

• ***Each other*** s'utilise lorsque l'on veut exprimer **une réciprocité** (= l'un et l'autre).

Exemple :

*Ted and Lucy looked at **each other**.*
(Ted looked at Lucy and Lucy looked at Ted.)
Ted et Lucy se sont regardés.

• Lorsque le sujet et l'objet se réfèrent à **la même personne**, on utilise alors les **pronoms réfléchis** : *myself, yourself, himself, herself, itself, ourselves, yourselves, themselves.*

Exemple :

*Ted said to **himself**, "What a great evening!"*
Ted s'est dit : "Quelle bonne soirée!"

▲ Complète les phrases soit avec un composé de *–self*, soit avec *each other*.

1. Mary looked at ... in the mirror.
2. We know ... very well, because we live next to ...
3. Selfish people only think of ...
4. Mark sometimes composes songs: it's a way to express ...
5. We really enjoyed ... at the concert.
6. Ann and I often help ... with our homework.
7. We recite our lessons to ... ; she recites her lessons to me, and I do the same.

Réutilise tes connaissances

1 Dis en anglais.

1. Hier j'ai vu mon professeur d'anglais pendant que je faisais des courses avec ma mère.
2. Est-ce que tu as regardé le film hier soir?
3. Regarde-toi dans la glace.
4. Ils se sont dit au revoir.

2 Imagine une suite ou un début aux phrases suivantes.

1. Last week we ...
2. While we were doing a test, ...
3. ... when all of a sudden ...
4. As soon as they saw each other, ...

2 A trip through the USA

Objectifs

1— *so, so much, so many*
There are so many skyscrapers!
Le style indirect :
les questions au style indirect

2— Le *present perfect*
This is the first time I've been to ...

3— La similitude, la différence
Carrie is on vacation ...
So is Jeff.

The first settlers

1607
First English settlers in Jamestown, Virginia.

1620
The Pilgrim Fathers – Englishmen hoping to find religious freedom – arrived at Plymouth, Massachusetts.

An independent nation

4th July, 1776
Declaration of Independence.
The English colonies became the thirteen original states of the United States of America.

1789
George Washington: the first President of the United States.

How much do you know about the United States of America?

QUIZ

Look at the maps and read the information.
Then do the quiz in your workbook. ▸ **WB, p. 20**

population: 290 million inhabitants

surface area: Texas is as big as France.
The United States is seventeen times as big as France.

The Civil War

▶ **1861-1865**
Eleven Southern states refused to abolish slavery. They declared their independence. But in 1865, the North defeated the South and abolished slavery all over the country.

▶ **1865**
President Abraham Lincoln's assassination.

The Great Depression

▶ **1929**
The stock market crashed and 10 million Americans lost their jobs.

▶ **1933**
President Franklin D. Roosevelt created the slogan "A new deal for the American people".

WWII

▶ **1941**
After the Japanese attack on Pearl Harbour the US entered WWII.

▶ **1945**
The US dropped two atomic bombs on the Japanese cities of Hiroshima and Nagasaki.

The years of protest

▶ **The 60s**
Vast demonstrations against the war in Vietnam and against racial segregation.

▶ **1963**
President J.F. Kennedy's assassination.

Nine-eleven

▶ **9-11-2001**
On September 11th, 2001, two hijacked planes crashed into the Twin Towers of the World Trade Center in New York City. These skyscrapers were destroyed in a few minutes.

1 There are so many skyscrapers!

Review

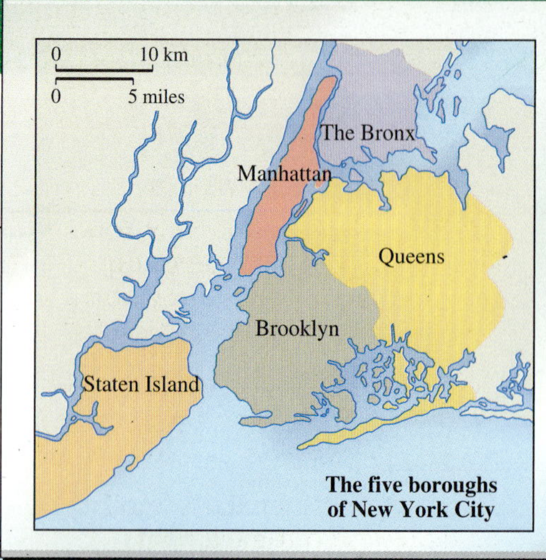

The five boroughs of New York City

1. Ask questions. ▶ WB, pp. 22-23

A group of tourists is visiting New York. Imagine the questions they ask their guide. Use the suggestions in the boxes and begin your questions with:

How ... much / many / hot / cold / long / far / high / old

New York City
- number of boroughs?
  - of inhabitants?
  - of nationalities?
- temperature
  - in January?
  - in July?

Manhattan

The Statue of Liberty
- age?
- height?
- weight?
- length of its arm?
  - of its index?
  - of its nose?
- distance from Manhattan?
- time to get there?

The Empire State Building
- height?
- number of floors?
  - of steps?
  - of elevators?
- time to get to the top?
- price of a ticket?
- number of people working inside?

2. Pairwork. ▸ WB, p. 24

You are talking about New York. You (A) start a dialogue using the elements in the yellow box. Your partner (B) answers using:

so + adjective

so much + singular

so many + plural

Then your partner starts another dialogue using the elements in the blue box and you answer.

- *lots of yellow cabs*
- *a lot of traffic*
- *streets / crowded*
- *lots of theaters*
- *hotels / expensive*
- *Central Park / big*
- *lots of shops open all night*

A: *There are **lots of yellow cabs**, aren't there?*

B: *Yes, there are. I didn't know there were **so many yellow cabs**.*

- *view from the plane / spectacular*
- *a lot of wind*
- *lots of tourists*
- *skyscrapers / high*
- *a lot of noise*
- *lots of museums*
- *Broadway / long*

B: *The **view from the plane** is **spectacular**, isn't it?*

A: *Yes, it is. I didn't know it was **so spectacular**.*

3. Reported speech.

Do you remember the different questions the tourists asked their guide? Make more comments about their questions, as in this example:

How long does it take to get to the top?

*The tourists **want to know** / **ask** **how long** it takes to get to the top.*

Then, do the task in your workbook. ▸ WB, pp. 24-25

Listening

1. Listening comprehension.

Listen to the conversation and do the task in your workbook. ▸ WB, p. 26

2. Summary.

Now, sum up the story with the help in your workbook. ▸ WB, p. 26

Oral practice

L'accent de mot : le rôle de la terminaison *-ion*

■ Ecoute et repère les syllabes accentuées dans les mots suivants :

• *conversation* • *information*
• *declaration* • *million*
• *segregation* • *demonstration*

Quelle règle peux-tu tirer?

■ Fais l'exercice d'entraînement dans ton *workbook*. ▸ WB, p. 25

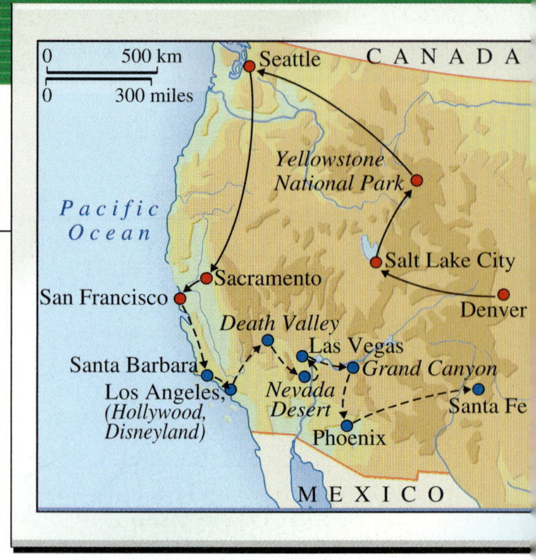

Review

2 This is the first time I've been to the West Coast!

1. Look and comment. ▸ WB, p. 27

A group of tourists is visiting the Western States. Look at the map and say where *they **have** already **been** to* (places marked •) and where *they **haven't been** to yet* (places in marked •).

2. Make dialogues. ▸ WB, pp. 27-28

Ted and Mary are tourists. For Ted, every experience is a new one, whereas for Mary it's not.

Look at the information about Mary and make dialogues using the verbs given as in this example:

TED: *"This is the first time I**'ve gambled**! **Have** <u>you</u> **gambled** before?"*

MARY: *"Yes I **have**! I **gambled** two years ago when I was in Atlantic City."*

TED	MARY
Las Vegas 	Atlantic City, two years ago — [gamble]
Death Valley 	Mexico, last year — [see a rattlesnake] the Sahara, in 1999 — [drive through the desert]
the Grand Canyon 	Niagara Falls — [fly in a helicopter] the Canadian Rockies — [hike down a canyon]

TED	MARY
	Hawaii, last summer — [surf in the Pacific] New Zealand — [swim in the Pacific]

3. Listen and comment. ▸ WB, p. 28

Listen to the recording and choose the right answer using:
It's the first time / It's not the first time ...

Listening

1. Listening comprehension.

Listen to the conversation and do the task in your workbook.
▸ WB, p. 29

2. Summary.

Now, sum up the story with the help in your worbook.
▸ WB, p. 29

Oral practice

Les pronoms personnels accentués

■ Les mots «outils» tels que les pronoms personnels, les auxiliaires, les articles, les prépositions, ne sont généralement pas accentués.
Exemple :
<u>This</u> is the <u>first</u> <u>time</u> I've <u>gambled</u>.
(Les mots soulignés sont ceux qui sont accentués).

■ Si on accentue un pronom personnel, cela correspond à une mise en relief: à l'oral, le pronom est prononcé sur un ton plus aigu; à l'écrit, il est souligné ou mis en italiques.
Exemple :
Have <u>you</u> gambled before?
signifie « Et vous, avez-vous déjà joué dans un casino?»
Ainsi, les expressions comme «moi, je ...» etc. ne se traduisent jamais, comme en français, par un double pronom (~~*me*~~, *I*) mais par l'intonation (*<u>I</u>*).

■ Fais l'exercice d'entraînement dans ton *workbook*. ▸ WB, pp. 28-29

Basics

3 Carrie is on vacation in the South. So is Jeff.

Carrie and Jeff, two American students, are visiting the South during their summer vacation. They have just met in a youth hostel in New Orleans.

1. Listen and speak. ▸ WB, p. 30

Carrie and Jeff realize that they have a lot in common: what is true for her is true for him.
First, say how they are alike.
Then, try to imagine reasons why, as in these examples:

*Carrie **is** on vacation in the South.* → ***So is** Jeff.*
He has always wanted to visit the South.

*She **hasn't** been to the South before.* → ***Neither has** Jeff.*
He couldn't afford it.

1. She is planning to go to a jazz band concert in New Orleans.
2. She was surprised to hear a lot of French words in Louisiana.
3. She didn't finish her Cajun dinner, it was too spicy.
4. She visited some old houses in New Orleans.
5. She wants to go on a cruise on the Mississippi.
6. She hasn't seen a cotton field in Alabama yet.
7. She can't afford to stay more than a week.
8. She would like to see alligators and water snakes in the bayous in Louisiana.
9. She won't have time to see Martin Luther King's birthplace in Atlanta.
10. She will probably visit Elvis Presley's house in Memphis.

2. Make comments. ▸ WB, p. 31

They have met another student, Laura, who is from Baton Rouge. She has nothing in common with Carrie and Jeff: what is true for them isn't true for her. Using the information from the ten sentences above express this idea as in these examples:

*Carrie and Jeff **are** on vacation in the South.* → *Laura **isn't**.*
*Carrie and Jeff **haven't been** to the South before.* → *Laura **has**.*

3. Listen and speak. ▸ WB, p. 31

Listen to someone talking about himself.
Compare yourself with him.

You hear:	You say:		
I love travelling.	***So do I!***	or	*I don't!*
I've never been to the United States.	***Neither have I!***	or	*I have!*

4. Listening comprehension. → Test

City life on either side of the Atlantic ▸ WB, p. 32

In the United States ...	In Great Britain ...	
junior high school	comprehensive school	*collège*
grade [greɪd]	form	*classe (niveau)*
principal	head teacher	*principal*
college ['kɒlɪdʒ] / university	college / university [ˌju:nɪ'vɜ:sɪtɪ]	*"fac"*
downtown	town centre	*centre ville*
subway	underground	*métro*
elevator	lift	*ascenseur*
sidewalk	pavement	*trottoir*
highway	motorway ['məʊtəweɪ]	*autoroute*
truck [trʌk]	lorry	*camion*
cab / taxi	taxi	*taxi*
gas	petrol	*essence*
apartment	flat	*appartement*
neighborhood ['neɪbəhʊd]	neighbourhood	*quartier*
center	centre	*centre*
not ... either ['i:ðə] / neither	not ... either ['aɪðə] / neither	*non plus*

1. Listen and repeat.
Listen and repeat the words from the list.

2. Listen and answer.
Listen to the questions and give the right answer.

3. A hidden message.

reɪtʃəl ɪz ɪnˌθu:zɪ'æstɪk ə'baʊt 'gəʊɪŋ tə 'kɒlɪdʒ

Coin New Words

You can add a prefix to form the opposite of words.
Look at the following examples and find more adjectives and their opposites.

comfortable → uncomfortable
regular → irregular
patient → impatient
tolerant → intolerant

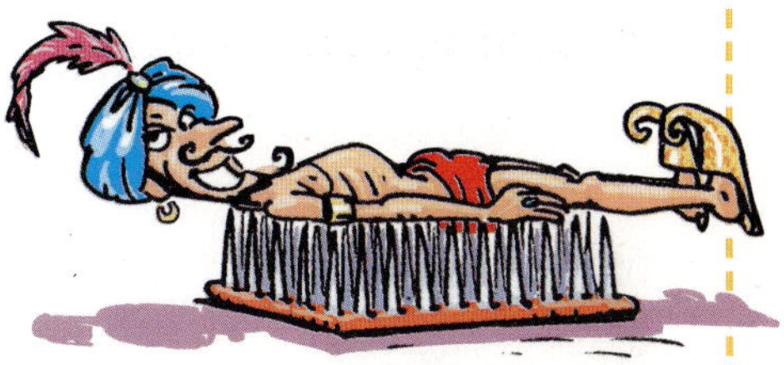

Now, do the exercise in your workbook. ▸ WB, p. 33

Topic

A school in Harlem

Emmanuel Kostakis is the Principal of a Junior High School in Harlem, in a neighborhood with drug and unemployment problems. 10% of the students of the school are Asian, 70% are Hispanic and 20% are Black. Listen to his interview.

▸ **WB, pp. 34-35**

1. Is Harlem really different from the rest of the city?

It's a world apart! Harlem is in Manhattan, **and yet** downtown Manhattan is such a different and inaccessible world! There are so many things that kids here can't have! That's why they feel a lot of anger and frustration.

2. How do they show this anger?

They fight. Fighting is part of their culture. Even parents say, "Don't hesitate to fight if you feel threatened". When they get touched, they have to touch back.

3. What do you mean?

Let's take an example: you are in a crowded corridor. Someone bumps into you. You want to show that you are tougher and not afraid. So does he. You don't want to lose face. Neither does he. So, you fight!

4. But your school has an excellent reputation. How do you explain this?

Yes, we are in Harlem, **and yet** this school has become a magnet school.

First, we specialize in what kids here need most: technology and computer science.

Secondly, we have zero tolerance for weapons, drugs (including cigarettes) and fighting. Any student who breaks the rules gets an automatic suspension. Always.

And thirdly, the students know that we are there for them. We understand that their attitude is often a sign of painful personal problems.

5. Do you feel you have succeeded?

Yes, I do! Absolutely! It's the first time that a school located in Harlem has attracted students from all over the city. There are very few drop-outs and many of our students have continued their studies and finished college. Many of them can say, "I've come a long way!"

and yet...

Harlem is in Manhattan, ...

... downtown Manhattan is such a different and inaccessible world!

Class work

Linking word. ▸ WB, p. 35

Read the caption under the two pictures above.
Then read the phrases in A and B about the United States, and connect them with *and yet*.

A

1. The official language in the US is English,
2. New York is bigger and more populated than Washington DC,
3. Most Americans favor strict gun control laws,
4. America is one of the richest countries in the world,

B

1. ... about 40 million Americans live under the poverty level.
2. ... Spanish is the mother tongue of millions of Americans.
3. ... it is not the capital city of the US.
4. ... half of the population has guns.

Role play.

Imagine you are one of the people you have just read about.
Follow your teacher's instructions.

What about you?

Answer the questions your teacher is going to ask about school life.

Discussion.

Do you agree or disagree?

Zero tolerance for weapons is a good thing.

Cigarettes are drugs.

Personal expression

Get ready for a talk.

Prepare a short talk comparing this school with yours, and your neighborhood with Harlem.

Your teacher may record you.

Writing task.

A student was caught fighting. The Principal has asked to see the student's father or mother.
Imagine what the three of them say in this scene. ▸ WB, p. 36

Listening → Test

More about...

... THE USA, A NATION OF IMMIGRANTS ▸ WB, p. 37

***All Americans** living in the United States now, except Native Americans, are immigrants or descendants of immigrants.*
The USA used to be called a "melting pot": a place where different cultures mixed and became American. But today, it is more of a mosaic: ethnic groups try to keep alive their own identities and traditions.

The first Native Americans (Amerindians) arrived on the North American continent 15,000 years ago. They came from Asia. Many of them died from diseases after their contact with Europeans or were massacred. Some tribes lost 90% of their population. They also lost their culture, their language and their religious customs. Their lands were confiscated and some tribes were deported or forced to live on arid land – reservations.

There are two million Indians today. They are now referred to as *Native Americans*.

The English founded the first thirteen colonies along the Atlantic coast during the 17th and 18th centuries. Their descendants are referred to as WASP's (White Anglo-Saxon Protestants).

In 1620, a hundred English men and women – the Pilgrims – went to America to find religious freedom. They sailed across the Atlantic on a ship, the *Mayflower*. When they arrived at Plymouth, Massachusetts, it was winter and extremely cold. Half of them died. The others survived thanks to Amerindians who helped them plant corn. After their first harvest the Pilgrims had a feast to give thanks to God. Thanksgiving, which commemorates this event, has become a national holiday celebrated by all Americans on the fourth Thursday of November.

Freedom from want by Norman Rockwell

Negroes for Sale.

A Cargo of very fine stout Men and Women, in good order and fit for immediate service, just imported from the Windward Coast of Africa, in the Ship Two Brothers.—
Conditions are one half Cash or Produce, the other half payable the first of January next, giving Bond and Security if required.
The Sale to be opened at 10 o'Clock each Day, in Mr. Bourdeaux's *Yard, at No. 48, on the Bay.*
May 19, 1784. JOHN MITCHELL.

The first Blacks were slaves. They were from West Africa: this is why the Blacks are now called *African Americans*. They were sold to Southern planters as early as the 17th century to work on cotton and tobacco fields.

Slavery was abolished in 1865 after the Civil War. It was only a hundred years later, thanks to the Civil Rights Movement led by Martin Luther King, that Blacks and Whites obtained equal rights.

Millions of European immigrants left their countries for political, economic or religious reasons. The first waves came in the late 1840s, during the Gold Rush, or during the Great Famine of Ireland. Many came from Germany, the Netherlands, and Scandinavia. Between 1880 and 1930 over 27 million immigrants, mainly Italians, Russians, Greeks and Jews from Eastern Europe, came to the United States. Until 1954 many of them passed through Ellis Island which is now a national monument.

The first Chinese immigrants arrived in San Francisco in the 1860s to build the transcontinental railroad which linked the west coast to the east coast.

After the war in Vietnam (mid-50s-1973) refugees from Vietnam, Laos and Cambodia settled in California.

A last wave of Asian immigrants came during the 1990s and settled mostly along the west coast, in Washington State and in California.

The Hispanics (or Latinos) are immigrants from Central and South America and the Caribbean. Many arrived in the 1960s.

The Hispanic community is now as large as the Black community. That is why there are so many newspapers, TV channels and radio programmes in Spanish throughout the United States. And in some cities, like Miami, it is more common to hear Spanish than English on the street.

Remember and Practise

1 *so, so much, so many*

1. **Un adjectif ou un adverbe** peut être modifié par divers adverbes : ***very, a bit, quite, so*** ...

Exemples :

*It's **very** expensive. It's **so** expensive.*
C'est très cher. C'est si cher.

2. ***Much*** peut modifier **un nom indénombrable** (= qui ne peut pas être précédé d'un nombre).

Exemple :

*How **much** time? So **much** time.*
Combien de temps ? Tellement de temps.

3. ***Many*** peut modifier **un nom dénombrable** (= qui peut être précédé d'un nombre).

Exemples :

*How **many** cars? So **many** cars.*
Combien de voitures ? Tellement de voitures.

There are so many skyscrapers!

▲ **Utilise *so, so much, so many* et le mot entre parenthèses pour donner des conseils dans les situations suivantes.**

The teacher gives us ten exercises every day. (homework)

→ *She shouldn't give us **so much** homework.*

1. Tom always goes to bed at 11 p.m. (late)
2. Arthur spends $10 a week on candies. (money)
3. Mr Guinness drinks four pints of beer a day. (alcohol)
4. Mary never tidies up her room. (messy)
5. Charles goes to fast food restaurants three times a week. (hamburgers)

2 Les questions au style indirect

1. **Question au style direct :**

Ordre des mots : WH- + aux. + sujet + verbe

Exemple :

*Mark asks, "Lucy, **where did you buy** your jeans?"*

2. **Question au style indirect :**

Ordre des mots : WH- + sujet + verbe

Exemple :

*Mark asks Lucy **where she bought** her jeans.*

3. **Remarque :**

Si la question ne comporte pas de mot interrogatif, elle est introduite par ***if*** au style indirect.

Exemple :

Mark asks, "Were they expensive?"
*He asks **if** they were expensive.*

They want to know how long it takes.

▲ **Rapporte au style indirect chaque phrase de ce dialogue, en commençant par *S/he asks, wants to know, answers, says*.**

Getting ready for a party.

Clara: Alex, are you ready?
What are you doing?

Alex: What time is it?

Clara: Nearly 8.00.

Alex: I want to bring the CD I've just bought.
I can't find it!
Where is it?
Have you seen it?

Clara: It's next to you, on your desk!
We're late! It's time to go!

3 *Present perfect* / prétérit

1. Le ***present perfect*** (auxiliaire *have* au présent + participe passé) s'utilise lorsque l'on fait le **bilan présent** de ses **expériences passées**.

Ainsi, l'expression *This is the first time* ... est suivie du *present perfect* car on passe en revue sa vie passée jusqu'au moment présent.

Exemple :

*This is the first time I **have seen** a rattlesnake.*
C'est la première fois que je vois un serpent à sonnette.

En français, contrairement à l'anglais, on utilise le présent.

2. Le **prétérit** s'emploie pour parler d'une **action passée coupée du présent** et dont **la date est mentionnée ou sous-entendue**.

Exemple :

*I **swam** in the Pacific three years ago.*
Il y a trois ans, j'ai nagé dans le Pacifique.

This is the first time I've been to the West Coast.

▲ **Complète les phrases en utilisant le prétérit, ou le *present perfect*.**

1. When ... the first thirteen colonies ... their independence? [declare]
2. I .... my keys again! It's the second time I ... them this week! [lose]
3. He ... through the desert before. [never drive]
4. We ... in a helicopter when we visited New York. [not fly]
5. ... you ever ... so many steps? [climb up]
6. Last summer we ... to the top of the Eiffel Tower. [climb]

4 La similitude / la différence

Pour exprimer la similitude («Moi aussi», «Moi non plus») ou la différence («Moi si», «Pas moi»), on construit des phrases brèves contenant un sujet et un auxiliaire comme pour les *question-tags* ou les réponses courtes.

Dans la phrase qui vient d'être dite il faut donc bien repérer: s'il y a un auxiliaire ou non, et le temps qui est utilisé.

Ces répliques se construisent selon les schémas suivants :

1. Pour exprimer une **similitude**:

- Après une phrase **affirmative**, on emploie:

So + auxiliaire + sujet

Exemple:

– *I* ***visited*** *New York last year.*
– ***So did I.*** (Moi aussi.)

- Après une phrase **négative**, on emploie:

Neither + auxiliaire + sujet

Exemple:

– *I'm* ***not*** *crazy about rodeos.*
– ***Neither am I.*** (Moi non plus.)

2. Pour exprimer une **différence**:

- Après une phrase **affirmative**, on emploie:

Sujet + auxiliaire négatif

Exemple:

– *I* ***want*** *to go to Disneyworld.*
– ***I don't!*** (Pas moi!)

- Après une phrase **négative**, on emploie:

Sujet + auxiliaire affirmatif

Exemple:

– *I've* ***never been to*** *Miami.*
– ***I have!*** (Moi si!)

Carrie is on vacation in the South. So is Jeff.

1 Imagine quelles phrases pourraient entraîner les répliques ci-dessous:

1. … – So can I.
2. … – So have I.
3. … – Neither did I.
4. … – So would I.
5. … – Neither do I.
6. … – I do!
7. … – I can't!
8. … – I have!
9. … – I won't!

2 Construis des phrases brèves exprimant la similitude ou la différence en fonction de ce qui est vrai pour toi.

1. "I don't know how deep the Grand Canyon is."
2. "I will go to the United States next year."
3. "I wouldn't like to find a rattlesnake in my tent."
4. "I've never seen a cotton field."
5. "I can't remember how many boroughs there are in New York City."
6. "I really enjoy visiting museums."
7. "I think that gambling is a dangerous habit."
8. "I found this exercise difficult."

Réutilise tes connaissances

1 Dis en anglais.

1. – Je ne savais pas que tant de villes américaines avaient des noms français.
   – Moi non plus.
2. – C'est la première fois que je prends un bateau sur le Mississippi.
   – Moi aussi.
3. – Je n'ai jamais mangé de nourriture cajun.
   – Moi si! Je suis allé dans un restaurant cajun la semaine dernière.
4. Miami est aux Etats-Unis, et pourtant beaucoup de gens parlent espagnol dans la rue et dans les lieux publics.

2 Imagine un début ou une suite aux phrases suivantes.

1. But Sir, you can't expel me! It's the first time …
2. I have never been to New York, and yet …
3. My father wants to know why …
4. Did you know that …
5. … and neither can French students.

3 Canada, a land of adventure

Objectifs

1— Les pronoms relatifs
People and things that shape Canada.

2— *let / make someone do ...*
Canada makes me dream.

Le style indirect avec *say / tell*

3— *used to*
The Inuit used to be called "Eskimos".

The Native Canadians

▶10,000 BC
Asian nomadic tribes travelling on foot from Siberia settled in North America. Their descendants are the Amerindian tribes and the Inuit. Now these groups are called "The First Nations". They make up about 4% of Canada's total population.

The French

▶1534
Jacques Cartier took possession of the area around the St. Lawrence River in the name of François I, King of France.

▶1608
Samuel de Champlain founded the city of Quebec as a base for fur trade with the Indians.

▶1663
Canada became a province of France.

How much do you know about Canada?

QUIZ

Look at the map and read the information.
Then do the quiz in your workbook. WB, p. 38

population: 28 million inhabitants
surface area: the second largest country in the world
currency: the Canadian dollar

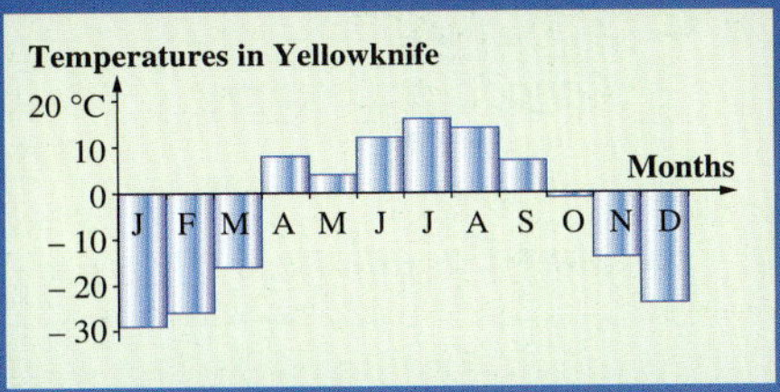

The British

The late 17th century
The British settled in Nova Scotia. Later, the Hudson's Bay Company – a British company – engaged in fur trade with the Indian tribes.

The British-French rivalry

1763
After a century of rivalry between the French and the English, France ceded Quebec to England. Quebec had a special status with French as the official language, whereas English was spoken in the rest of the country.

A new country

1867
Canada (population: 3.5 million inhabitants) obtained the right to have its own central government.

1885
Completion of the Canadian Pacific Railway (joining the east and west coasts).

1931
Canada became independent but joined the Commonwealth.

1965
A new flag replaced the British flag.

Canada today

After WWII
Canada attracted immigrants from all over the world.

1967
The World Fair took place in Montreal.
Canada celebrated its 100th anniversary.

1999
The Northwest Territories were divided and a new territory, Nunavut, was created. It has become a homeland for the Inuit.

1 People and things that shape Canada.

Review

Canada is a country	*which / that*	*has two official languages.*
	whose	*only neighbour is the USA.*
	Ø / (that)	*people visit for its natural beauty.*
Most Canadians	*who / that*	*live in Quebec speak French.*

1. Listen.

Listen to nine definitions and do the task in your workbook. ▸ WB, p. 40

the French

the English

a totem pole

Inuit people

Queen Elizabeth

a maple tree

ice hockey

a caribou

a beaver

2. Make comments. ▶ WB, p. 41

Now, turn back to pages 40 and 41 and talk about the following people, places or things using *who, which, that, whose, Ø.*

- Jacques Cartier is the French explorer ...
- The Hudson's Bay Company is a company ...
- Nunavut is the territory ...
- The Canadian Pacific Railway is the railway ...
- Quebec City is a city ...
- French is the language ...
- The First Nations are people ... ancestors ...

3. The day when ... ▶ WB, p. 41

*July 1st is **the day when** Canadians celebrate their national day.*
*1965 is **the year when** a new Canadian flag replaced the British flag.*

How well do you remember the history of Canada?
What do the following dates refer to?

• 1534 • 1663 • 1867• 1967 • 1999

Make answers beginning with:

*It's the year **when** ...*

4. What about you?

Try to remember the day when something unusual happened in class.
Ask questions as in this example:

Do you remember the day when Kevin fell asleep in class?

Listening

1. Listening comprehension.

Listen to the conversation and do the task in your workbook. ▶ WB, p. 42

2. Summary.

Now, sum up the story with the help in your workbook. ▶ WB, p. 42

Oral practice

L'accent de mot : le rôle de la terminaison *-ian*

■ Ecoute et repère les syllabes accentuées dans les paires de mots suivants :

Canada → Canadian
American → Amerindian
Italy → Italian
music → musician
beauty → beautician
mathematics → mathematician

Quelle règle peux-tu tirer?

■ Fais l'exercice d'entraînement dans ton *workbook.* ▶ WB, p. 41

Basics

2 Canada makes me dream.

1. Look and comment. ▸ **WB, p. 43**

Adrian is a camp counsellor in a summer camp in the Canadian Rockies.

Look at the pictures below, work in pairs and say:

- what he **made** the group **do**
- what he **let** / **didn't let** them **do**

as in this example:

A: *He **let** them **go** canoeing on the lake.*
B: *He **made** them **put on** their life jackets.*

2. Listen.

Listen to the recording and do the task in your workbook. ▸ **WB, p. 44**

3. What makes you laugh? ▸ WB, p. 44

One night, Adrian told the group a folk tale. Look at how some of them reacted.

It made her cry. *It made them laugh.* *It made her feel sleepy.*

What or who makes you dream / laugh / feel sleepy?
What makes you furious / sick?

4. Reported speech.

Look at the drawings on page 44 and make more comments about Adrian, using the verb *tell* as in these examples:

Adrian ***says:*** « *Go to bed!* »

He ***tells them*** *to go to bed.*

He ***says:*** « *Don't stay up late!* »

He ***tells them*** *not to stay up late.*

Then, do the task in your workbook. ▸ WB, pp. 44-45

Listening

1. Listening comprehension.

Listen to the conversation and do the task in your workbook. ▸ WB, pp. 45-46

2. Summary.

Now, sum up the story with the help in your workbook. ▸ WB, p. 46

Oral practice

Les consonnes qui disparaissent à l'oral

■ La consonne finale d'un mot peut être «absorbée» par celle du mot suivant lorsque celles-ci sont identiques.

Par exemple, dans la phrase *I want to go*, le *t* final du verbe *want* ne se prononce pas, il disparaît au profit du *t* de *to*.

Autres exemples :
- *a bad day*
- *he's sleeping*
- *don't drink cold water*
- *stop pushing*

■ Le même phénomène se produit avec les consonnes aux sons proches.
Ainsi la marque du prétérit – ou du participe passé en *–ed–* est peu ou pas audible dans certains cas.

Par exemple, dans les phrases suivantes:
They picked two flowers.
They stayed together.
le son [d] ou [t] de la terminaison du prétérit se confond avec le son [t] qui suit.

■ Fais l'exercice d'entraînement dans ton *workbook*. ▸ WB, p. 45

3 The Inuit used to be called "Eskimos".

1. What did the Inuit use to do? ▸ WB, pp. 47-48

Work in pairs to compare the way of life of the Inuit in the past with their way of life today, using the information below and the verbs in the box, as in this example:

A: ***In the past**, they **used to** travel by dogsled.*

B: ***Now** they **don't any more**. They travel by snowmobile.*

- *travel by …*
- *use … for transportation*
- *live*
- *get light from …*
- *hunt caribous with …*

IN THE PAST, …	NOW …

a dogsled

a snowmobile

oil lamps

igloos and tents

kayaks

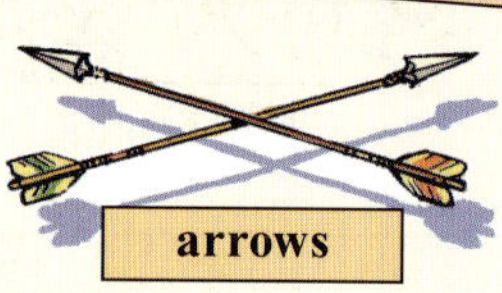

arrows

electric light bulbs

modern houses

rifles

a floatplane

2. What didn't the Inuit use to do? ▸ WB, p. 48

Make more comparisons between the past and now, using the information you are given in the box, as in this example:

A: *The Inuit **didn't use** to have an official language, did they?*

B: *No, they didn't. **But now** they have an official language: **Inuktitut**.*

- ***official language:** Inuktitut* [have]
- ***territory:** Nunavut* [have]
- ***airline company:** Inuit Air* [have]
- ***foreign languages:** English or French* [speak]
- ***food:** imported food* [buy]
- ***soft drinks:** Coke and other sodas* [drink]
- ***the outside world:** through the Internet* [to communicate with …]

3. What about you?

Talk about yourself when you were little: your habits, your physical appearance, your favourite TV programmes or games, your likes and dislikes.
Begin your sentences with:

*When I was little, I **used to** … / I **didn't use to** …*

4. Listening comprehension. → Test

SIGHTSEEING ▸ WB, p. 49

go sightseeing	*faire du tourisme*
guided tour ['gaɪdɪd 'tʊə]	*visite guidée*
museum [mjuː'zɪəm]	*musée*
art gallery [aːt 'gælərɪ]	*musée (de peintures, de sculptures)*
(summer) camp	*colonie de vacances*
theme park [θiːm paːk]	*parc à thème*
seaside resort ['siːsaɪd rɪ'zɔːt]	*station balnéaire*
winter sports	*sports d'hiver*
ski resort	*station de ski*

WILDLIFE ▸ WB, p. 49

wildlife ['waɪldlaɪf]	*la faune et la flore*
endangered species [ɪn'deɪndʒəd 'spiːʃiːz]	*espèce en voie de disparition*
extinct (species)	*(espèce) disparue*
WWF (World Wildlife Fund)	WWF

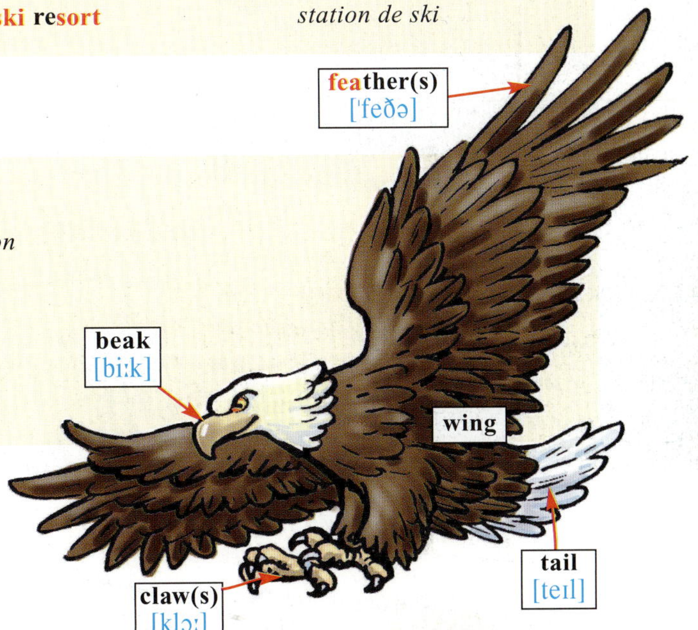

1. Listen and repeat.

Listen and repeat the words from the list.

2. Listen and answer.

Listen to the questions and give the right answer.

3. A hidden message.

ɪn'deɪndʒəd 'spiːʃiːz
ʃʊd biː mɔː prə'tektɪd

Coin New Words

Some adjectives are created by adding the suffix *-ful* or *–less*.
Look at the following examples:

beauty → **beautiful**	**success** → **successful**	**fright** → **frightful**
hope → **hopeless**	**mother** → **motherless**	**home** → **homeless**

Now do the exercise in your workbook. ▸ WB, p. 50

Topic

A FAMILY TRIP ACROSS CANADA

Gary and Rachel's parents gave each of them a diary so that they could write about things they saw, people they met and places they visited during their summer holiday across Canada. Here are three pages from Gary's diary. ▶ **WB, pp. 51-52**

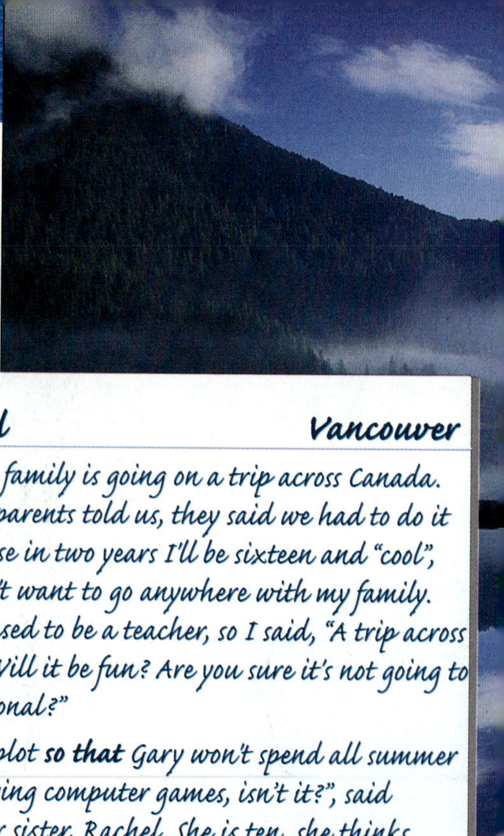

June 3rd — ***Vancouver***

Our whole family is going on a trip across Canada. When my parents told us, they said we had to do it now because in two years I'll be sixteen and "cool", and I won't want to go anywhere with my family. My mom used to be a teacher, so I said, "A trip across Canada? Will it be fun? Are you sure it's not going to be educational?"

"This is a plot ***so that*** *Gary won't spend all summer inside playing computer games, isn't it?", said my younger sister, Rachel. She is ten, she thinks she knows everything and she wants to know everything. "How far will we be going?", she asked. Dad answered, "You'll have to put up with your brother in the back seat of the car for 6,000 km". "How exciting!!!", she said, forcing a smile.*

July 12th — ***Yellowknife***

Yesterday we woke up early in the morning ***so that*** *we could enjoy the nice weather all day long. It was the best wildlife day! While we were canoeing, we first saw two moose. They raised their heads out of the water, plants hanging out of their mouths, and stared at us. They didn't seem very excited to see us! We also saw at least two bald eagles, a grizzly in the distance, and – the best sighting of the day – a lynx which was standing motionless near the river. It looked like an extremely large cat. It saw us, but it didn't move. We all stopped paddling. We watched the lynx and it watched us, until we rounded a bend and couldn't see it any more.*

July 30th — ***Bay of Fun***

When my parents are not making me learn about history, they're making me hike. And when they're not making me hike, they're making me eat fish, I mean real fish with head, tail, and ... eyes! Ugh! This morning we went to Grand Pré, a historic site where the French-speaking Acadians used to live. Mum told us about the tragic events that took place there. In 1755 the British burnt their villages, and the Acadians were scattered far and wide. Friends and families never saw each other again, ever. Rachel got furious about it. I told her to simmer down, it all happened a million years ago ... well ... 250 years ago. "It's still not right!", she yelled. Phew! Take cover when Rachel gets upset.

Thank God, tomorrow there will be absolutely no history, no hiking, no fish ... we're going whale-watching! Wow!!!

We woke up early in the morning... *we could enjoy the nice weather all day long.*

Class work

Linking word. ▸ WB, p. 52

Read the caption under the two pictures above.
Then read the phrases in A and B about Canada, and connect them with *so that*.

A
1. Polar bears are protected ...
2. Montreal has an "underground city" ...
3. All official documents are bilingual ...
4. On icy roads, Canadians use sand – and not salt – ...

B
1. ... the soil won't get polluted.
2. ... people can shop in the winter without going outside.
3. ... they won't become extinct.
4. ... all Canadian citizens can understand them.

Role play.

Imagine you are one of the people you have just read about.
Follow your teacher's instructions.

What about you?

Answer the questions your teacher is going to ask about spending holidays with adults.

Discussion.

Do you agree or disagree?

Long trips are a bore!

Zoos are a good thing.

Personal expression

Get ready for a talk.

Imagine you have won a trip to Canada. Prepare a short talk and explain where you would like or wouldn't like to go.

Your teacher may record you.

Writing task.

Something made you furious / sad / happy today.
Write a page in an imaginary diary.
▸ WB, p. 53

Listening
→ Test

More about...

... NATURE AND CULTURE IN CANADA

▸ WB, pp. 54-55

The Northern Lights *(aurora borealis)* sometimes light up the sky in the North of Canada from September to October and from March to April. The sky becomes pink, green or even bright red or yellow.

Whales, from the smallest – killer whales, or orcas – to the largest – blue whales – , feed on krill at the meeting of the Saguenay and St. Lawrence rivers, in Quebec. The best period to go whale-watching is between August and October, but you can watch beluga whales all year round.

Polar bears migrate to Hudson Bay at the beginning of the cold season to fish seals from under the ice. They go through the town of Churchill which calls itself "The Polar Bear Capital of the World". Bears sometimes try to enter people's homes looking for food.

They are very dangerous animals and tourists who want to go bear-viewing take special high vehicles called "tundra buggies".

All these inventions are Canadian.

- The system of **time zones** was imagined in the 1890s during the building of the Canadian Pacific Railway.
- The game of ***Trivial Pursuit*, instant mashed potatoes, the zipper, the snowmobile**, and **the cardiac pacemaker** are also Canadian inventions.
- Last but not least: ... **basketball**. It was invented in 1891 by a Canadian Physical Education instructor who wanted to find a good way for his students to get exercise indoors during the long Canadian winters.

Montreal, with two thirds of the population speaking French, is the largest French-speaking city outside Paris.

To escape the harsh winter, there is an "underground city", where you can shop, eat out, see a movie or go from building to building without going outside.

Toronto, in Ontario, has 3 million inhabitants and is the largest city in Canada. It is also the most ethnically diverse city in the world, with Greek, Portuguese, Chinese, Italian and Ukrainian communities, and even a "Little India".

One of the symbols of Toronto is the CN Tower (583 metres high) with its glass elevator outside of the tower and its glass floor which lets you see through it, 500 metres down. Not for those who are afraid of heights!

Edmonton, in Alberta, is one of the most popular tourist sites in Canada because of its huge shopping mall - actually the largest in the world, with 800 stores, an amusement park, the biggest indoor water park in the world that includes a pool complex with slides, waves and an artificial beach. It also has a mini-golf course, an ice rink, cinemas and restaurants. It's so big that you can even rent a little scooter to get around!

Vancouver, in British Columbia, is built on a bay on the Pacific coast and is surrounded by high mountains. Its inhabitants can go skiing in winter and canoeing in summer.

Following the retrocession of Hong Kong to China in 1999, a lot of wealthy Chinese emigrated to Vancouver, boosting the economy and increasing an already large Asian community. One third of the population of the city is Chinese.

All these famous film stars are Canadian.

- **Keanu Reeves** (*Matrix, Dracula ...*) spent his childhood in Toronto. That is where **Jim Carrey** (*The Mask, The Truman Show...*) began acting.
- **Michael J. Fox** (*Back to the Future, Spin City*) started his career in a Canadian television series.
- And **Pamela Anderson** (*Baywatch*) was born on Vancouver Island.

1 Les pronoms relatifs

People and things that shape Canada.

1. On forme des phrases complexes à partir de phrases simples en les reliant par des **pronoms relatifs**. Le pronom relatif se réfère à l'antécédent mentionné dans la proposition principale.

Le choix du pronom relatif dépend de la nature de **l'antécédent** (humain ou non humain) et de **sa fonction** dans la subordonnée (sujet, complément ou complément de nom).

Tableau simplifié des pronoms relatifs

fonction	pronom relatif sujet	pronom relatif complément	pronom relatif complément de nom
antécédent humain	**who / that** *Most Canadians who / that live in Quebec speak French.*	**Ø / (that)** *The girl Ø you met is from Toronto.*	**whose** *Amerindians are people whose ancestors came from Asia.*
antécédent non humain	**which / that** *Canada is a country which / that has few inhabitants.*	**Ø / (that)** *The clothes Ø they wear are very warm.*	**whose** *Canada is a country whose only neighbour is the USA.*

2. Remarques :

• *that* disparaît généralement lorsqu'il est complément (direct ou indirect) du verbe.

Exemple :

*The clothes **Ø** they wear are very warm.*
Les vêtements qu'ils portent sont très chauds.

• Avec les relatifs Ø ou *that*, la préposition est rejetée après le verbe.

Exemple :

*The friend I play hockey **with** is from Calgary.*
L'ami avec qui je joue au hockey est de Calgary.

• Alors qu'en français « où » peut avoir un sens temporel (le moment/le jour où...), en anglais, on utilise ***when*** qui a alors un rôle de relatif.

Exemple :

*Do you remember the day **when** we first met?*
Tu te souviens du jour où nous nous sommes rencontrés pour la première fois ?

▲ **Inclus chaque deuxième phrase sous forme de proposition relative après le groupe nominal en italiques.**

1. *The maple leaf* is the symbol of Canada.
   It is on the Canadian flag.
2. *My cousins* have asked for a work permit.
   They want to work in Montreal.
3. In this restaurant, *the maple syrup* is delicious.
   They serve it with pancakes.
4. *This guide-book* will be useful for my trip.
   I bought it yesterday.
5. *The wood cabin* was not very comfortable.
   We rented it for a week.
6. *This writer* is only 24 years old.
   Her last novel has become a best-seller.

2 let / make someone do ...

Canada makes me dream.

Les verbes ***make*** et ***let*** se construisent ainsi :

Sujet 1 + ***make / let*** + sujet 2 + base verbale

Si le sujet 2 est un pronom, il est sous forme de complément (*me, you, him, her, us, them*).

1. ***make*** exprime l'idée qu'**une influence** plus ou moins forte est **exercée** sur quelqu'un (véritable contrainte ou simple effet produit).

Exemples :

*He **made** his son **wear** a helmet.*
Il a obligé son fils à porter un casque.

*Canada **makes** me **dream**.*
Le Canada me fait rêver.

2. ***let*** exprime l'idée de **permission donnée (ou refusée)** à quelqu'un.

Exemple :

*He **didn't let** us **swim**.*
Il ne nous a pas laissés nager.

▲ **Reformule les phrases suivantes en utilisant *let* ou *make*.**

1. The instructor didn't want them to go rafting without life jackets.
2. When I read *The Call of the Wild*, I cried a lot.
3. Because of the bad weather, they stayed indoors.
4. He ate raw fish and he felt sick.
5. Tom's parents don't allow him to drive their snowmobile.
6. When she goes swimming, she feels relaxed.
7. Do your teachers allow you to chew gum in class?

3 Le style indirect avec *say / tell*

He tells them to go to bed.

Le verbe français « dire » peut se traduire en anglais soit par *say*, soit par *tell*.

1. **Au style direct**, on utilise toujours ***say*** :

Exemple:

*She **says**, "I'm fine. Don't worry!"*
Elle dit : « Je vais bien. Ne t'inquiète pas! »

2. **Au style indirect**, on utilise ***say*** ou ***tell***.

• Lorsque **la personne** à qui l'on parle **n'est pas mentionnée**, on utilise le verbe ***say***.

Exemple :

*She **says** (that) she is fine.*
Elle dit qu'elle va bien.

• Lorsque la **personne** à qui l'on parle **est mentionnée**, on utilise, en général, le verbe ***tell***. C'est pourquoi c'est ce verbe qui est utilisé lorsqu'on rapporte un **ordre** donné à quelqu'un.

Exemples :

*She **tells him** (that) she is fine.*
Elle lui dit qu'elle va bien.

*She **tells** him **not to** worry and **to** calm down.*
Elle lui dit de ne pas s'inquiéter et de se calmer.

▲ Raconte ce dialogue au style indirect en introduisant chaque phrase par *say* ou *tell*.

Peter: We're lost!
I don't know where we are.

Sue: Don't panic!
Give me the map!

Peter: You have got it.
Look in your bag!

Sue: I can't see anything.
Peter, give me the torch, please.

Peter: ... I left it in our tent.

Sue : Oh, Peter, you really are a pain!

4 Ce qui était vrai autrefois

The Inuit used to be called "Eskimos".

1. Pour mettre en relief qu'**un fait était vrai autrefois** mais ne l'est plus, on utilise ***used to / didn't use to*** suivi de la base verbale.

Exemples :

*Where **did** the Inuit **use to** live?*
Où habitaient les Inuit (autrefois) ?

*They **used to** live in igloos.*
(Autrefois) ils habitaient dans des igloos.

*They **didn't use to** live in houses.*
(Autrefois) ils n'habitaient pas dans des maisons.

2. Pour dire qu'autrefois il y avait ou qu'il n'y avait pas quelque chose, on utilise donc l'expression ***there used to be ... / there didn't use to be ...***

▲ Complète les phrases avec *used to / didn't use to* suivi d'un verbe.

1. Nunavut is independent, but it ... a part of the Northwest Territories.
2. Now, people travel a lot. In the past, they ... so much.
3. I like sport now, but when I was younger, I ... it.
4. There ... a lot more animal and plant species, but some of them have disappeared.
5. In those days, it was easy to find a job. There ... so much unemployment.

Réutilise tes connaissances

▲1 Dis en anglais.

1. Où sont les fleurs que tu as cueillies ?
2. Ma mère me fait ranger ma chambre toutes les semaines.
3. Mes parents ne me laissent pas passer la nuit chez des copains.
4. C'est le nounours avec lequel je dormais quand j'étais petit(e).
5. Avant, j'avais les cheveux blonds.

▲2 Imagine un début aux phrases suivantes.

1. ... who is famous all over the world.
2. ... which makes me dream.
3. ... whose beak is very sharp.
4. ... , but now I'm not any more.
5. ... , but now I do.

4 Let's go to Hollywood!

OBJECTIFS

1— La voix passive
A story that was adapted for the screen.

Le style indirect :
la concordance des temps

2— La voix passive avec les verbes *ask, give, tell, offer, show*
When a secretary is asked to put money in a safe ...

3— Le gérondif après les prépositions
Special effects are created by using a bagful of tricks.

How much do you know about the cinema?

Q U I Z

Look at the documents and read the information.
Then do the quiz in your workbook. ▸ **WB, p. 56**

The birth of motion pictures

▸1895
The French Lumière Brothers improved on Edison's kinetoscope and invented the *cinématographe*, which was both a camera and a projector.

▸1897
The first cinema opened in Paris. Films were simply scenes of moving images – trains, parades, waterfalls … Georges Meliès, a French magician, introduced the idea of storytelling in films and was the first to use special effects.

Silent films

▸The 1900s
There were 10,000 cinemas in the United States. An enormous amount of silent films was produced. Most were very short, lasting only a few minutes. In addition to a musical accompaniment, piano playing for example, live actors sometimes improvised the dialogues.

Hollywood's Golden Age

▸The 20s
Producers left for California where constant sunlight and varied landscapes (mountain, sea and desert) made it possible to shoot all types of films. Hollywood became the film-making capital.

▸1927
Introduction of sound in the *Jazz Singer*, the first "talkie".

▸1935
Introduction of colour.

The television age

▸In the 60s
With the increasing popularity of television, Hollywood's Golden Age came to an end. Films began to reflect the social changes of the times: some films criticized American attitudes towards Native Americans, (*Little Big Man,* 1970) or the US army intervention in Vietnam (*Apocalypse Now,* 1979).

The computer age

▸Since the early 80s
Computers have made it possible to manipulate images and to create characters and things that seem real. The technique of morphing, in which objects change form before the viewers' eyes, was first used in *Terminator II* (1990).

Review

1 A story that was adapted for the screen.

1. Tell the story. ▸ WB, pp. 58-59

The Addams Family was originally a comic strip. In 1991, Barry Sonnenfeld – who later directed *Men In Black* – adapted it as a mock horror film.

Read the beginning of the story.

Then, look at the drawings and continue telling the story.

A crook, whose name is Gordon, and his mother are interested in a treasure hidden in the Addams' mansion. On a dark stormy night, Gordon knocks at their door disguised as Fester, their long-lost uncle ...

- *A hand, whose name is Thing,* ***opens*** *the door.*
- *The door* ***is opened*** *by a hand, whose name is Thing.*

[open] 1

- The Addams … Gordon to dinner.
- Gordon ... to dinner.

[invite] 2

- He ... to see the treasure.

[take] 3

- Their daughter ... Gordon …
- Gordon ... their daughter ...

[accuse ... of being a fake] 4

- Morticia ... him to his ancestors.
- He ... to his ancestors.

[introduce] 5

- The Addams ... a big party.
- A big party ... the Addams.

[organize] 6

- The gentle monsters ... Gordon's life.
- Gordon's life ... the gentle monsters.

[change] 7

- A hurricane ... Gordon's nasty mother.
- Gordon's nasty mother ... a hurricane.

[blow away] 8

- The Addams ... Gordon …
- Gordon ... the Addams …

[accept ... as a member of the family] 9

2. What must be done? ▶ WB, p. 59

Imagine a director wants to shoot a film that takes place in the 19th century.

Look at the first picture and find out
- *what **must be** done*
- *what **is being** done.*

Then look at the second picture and find out
- *what **has been** done*
- *what **will be** done later.*

• telephone box • TV aerial • satellite dish
• billboard • no parking sign • traffic light
• traffic • door • tag • empty cans • can of paint

• remove • erase • hide • cut off • paint

3. Reported speech. ▶ WB, p. 60

Look at the drawings of *The Addams Family* on page 56 and make more comments.

*I **don't** trust him!*
*I **can't** believe him.*
*He**'s** a fake!*

*The daughter **told** her parents / **said** that she **didn't** trust him.*
*that she **couldn't** believe him.*
*that Gordon **was** a fake.*

Listening

1. Listening comprehension.

Listen to the conversation and do the task in your workbook. ▶ WB, pp. 61-62

2. Summary.

Now, sum up the story with the help in your workbook. ▶ WB, p. 62

Oral practice

Les terminaisons -er / -or

■ Ecoute et repère l'accentuation des mots suivants :

- *write → writer*
- *act → actor*
- *direct → director*
- *compose → composer*
- *design → designer*
- *produce → producer*

Quelle règle peux-tu tirer ?

■ Fais l'exercice d'entraînement dans ton *workbook.* ▶ WB, p. 61

2 When a secretary is asked to put money in a safe ...

• **leading role:** Anthony Perkins
• **characteristics:**
- in black and white - turning point in thrillers

1. Comment. ▸ WB, p. 63

Use the information you are given to comment on *Psycho*, one of the most famous American thrillers.

- *shoot (in ...)*
- *direct (by ...)*
- *play (by ...)*
- *consider (as ...)*

2. Listen.

Listen to the beginning of the story and do the task in your workbook. ▸ WB, p. 63

3. Continue the story. ▸ WB, pp. 63-64

Use the verbs given in the boxes A, B, C and D to continue the story.

In part A, begin each sentence with *"Marion"*; in part C, begin with "Norman", as in this example:

*Marion **is given** the key to her room.*

In parts B and D, complete the text.

A

- *ask*
- *give*
- *tell*
- *show*
- *offer*

B **And then ...**

While she is having a shower, she ... to death by a mysterious old woman.
Norman ... the shower and ... the body.
A detective ... by Marion's boss to find out what happened. Norman's behaviour seems strange and he and his mother ...

- *clean*
- *get rid of*
- *hire*
- *stab*
- *suspect*

C

- *ask*
- *show*

D **And then ...**

As the detective is climbing up the stairs in Norman's house, he ... by an old woman.
The key to the mystery ... at the end of the film when the mother ... in the cellar.

- *discover*
- *kill*
- *reveal*

4. How do they look?

What can you say about Marion? Marion's sister? the Bates' house? the policeman?

Use the adjectives in the box as in this example:

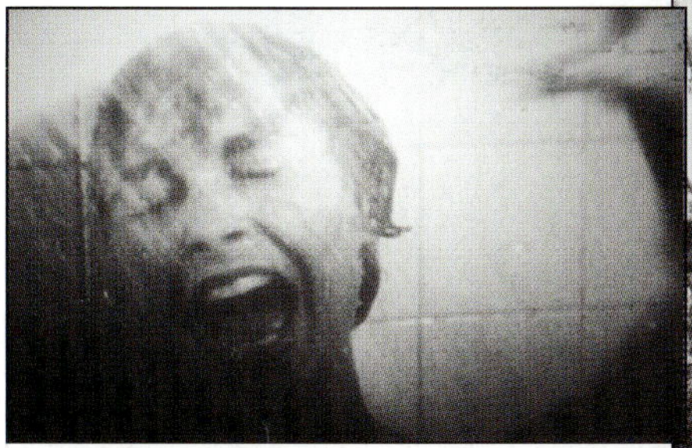

*Marion **looks** terrified.*

- *terrified*
- *haunted*
- *spooky*
- *frightening*
- *suspicious*
- *worried*

5. How do they sound?

Listen to different people talking and say how they sound, using the adjectives in the box, as in this example:

*She **sounds** angry.*

- *angry*
- *upset*
- *disappointed*
- *puzzled*
- *terrified*

Listening

1. Listening comprehension.

Listen to the conversation and do the task in your workbook. ▶ **WB, p. 65**

2. Summary.

Now, sum up the story with the help in your workbook. ▶ **WB, p. 65**

Oral practice

La forme en *-ing* / la forme passive en *-en*

■ L'auxiliaire *be* permet de construire deux formes: la forme en *-ing* et la forme passive. Lorsqu'un verbe a un participe passé en *-en*, la différence entre ces deux formes n'est pas toujours clairement perçue à l'oral.

Ecoute et répète les verbes suivants:

- *give: giving / given*
- *take: taking / taken*
- *eat: eating / eaten*
- *fall: falling / fallen*
- *see: seeing / seen*

■ A l'oral, le contexte et la logique de la phrase permettent de reconnaître la bonne forme.

Exemples:

- *He was* [ˈteɪkn] / [ˈteɪkɪŋ] *to see the treasure.*

La forme *taking* étant impossible pour des raisons grammaticales, seule la forme passive est possible: *He was taken.*

- *Gordon is* [ˈiːtn] / [ˈiːtɪŋ].

La logique du contexte permet de reconnaître la forme en *-ing*: *He is eating* (Gordon n'est pas mangé!).

■ Fais l'exercice d'entraînement dans ton *workbook.* ▶**WB, p. 64**

❸ Special effects are created by using a bagful of tricks.

Some special effects are created with computers, but many are still created by using traditional methods which are simpler, cheaper and faster.

1. What does it sound like? ▸ WB, p. 66

Listen and say what you think you hear, as in this example:
*It **sounds like** a heart beating.*

2. What does it look like? ▸ WB, pp. 66-67

Look and say what each drawing looks like, as in this example:
*In number 1, it **looks like** fog.*

3. How are these effects created? ▸ WB, p. 67

With a partner, use the information in the box to make dialogues, as in this example:

A: ***How** is the effect of fog created?*
B: *It is created **by** dropp**ing** dry ice into boiling water.*

Now, can you say how some special effects in *Men In Black II* were created? Use the information given in the box below.

- *spread salt and flour over the set*
- *drop dry ice* (neige carbonique) *into boiling water*
- *add effervescent aspirin to beer*
- *put food colouring into mashed potatoes*
- *mix coffee, syrup and food colouring*
- *use a huge fan*

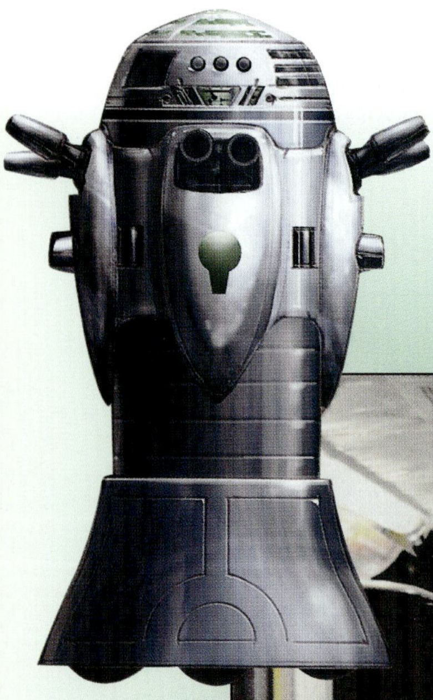

- *make rubber masks*
- *use radio-controlled robots*
- *manipulate puppets*
- *use CGI (Computer Generated Images)*

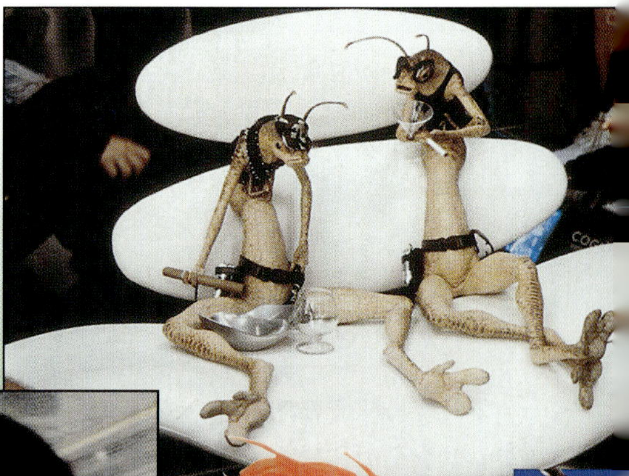

4. Listening comprehension. → Test

More Words

THE MAKING OF A FILM

▸ WB, p. 68

direct	*mettre en scène*	**part / role**	*rôle*
director	*metteur en scène*	**dub** [dʌb]	*doubler (en langue étrangère)*
producer	*producteur*	**screen**	*écran*
shoot, shot, shot	*tourner (un film)*	**sound effect**	*effet sonore*
shot	*prise de vue*	**soundtrack**	*bande son*
film (GB) / **movie** (US)	*film*	**thriller** ['θrɪlə]	*film à suspense*
set	*plateau de tournage*	**blockbuster**	*film à gros budget*
cast	*ensemble des acteurs*	**masterpiece**	*chef d'oeuvre*
credits	*générique*	**subtitle** ['sʌbtaɪtl]	*sous-titre; sous-titrer*
extra	*figurant*		
character ['kærəktə]	*personnage*		

1. Listen and repeat.

Listen and repeat the words from the list.

2. Listen and answer.

Listen to the questions and give the right answer.

3. A hidden message.

məʊst əv hɪz fɪlmz wɜː 'θrɪləz

Coin New Words

Some nouns are created by adding the suffix *–ness*.
Look at the following examples:

busy → **business**　　**kind** → **kindness**
thick → **thickness**　　**soft** → **softness**

Now, do the exercise in your workbook. ▸ WB, p. 68

What is it like to be a film star?

▸ WB, pp. 69-70

Kate Winslet has always wanted to be an actress. Her parents sent her to an exclusive private theatre school. But she was overweight and not wealthy. **As a result**, she was called names and rejected by her classmates.

Kate Winslet's on-screen romance with Leonardo DiCaprio in *Titanic* made her a star but she was determined not to get sucked into the crazy Hollywood machine. Soon, the British tabloids began suggesting that she was refused roles because she was not supermodel-thin. But Winslet said, “You don’t have to be a stick insect to be a successful actor! I am who I am! It seems to me that a lot of people who are thin are really unhappy.”

Brad Pitt was chosen by *People magazine* as one of the fifty most beautiful people in the world. He was even given the title of the Sexiest Man Alive. No wonder so many fans, especially girls and young women, want to know all about him.

For instance, during the shooting of a film, a local radio station even offered prizes for anyone who managed to steal something belonging to the actor.

How does he cope with all this?

“I don't want people to know about me”, he declared. “I don't know a thing about my favourite actors. I don't think you should.”

He is determined to control the effects of fame by protecting his privacy.

He doesn't let photographers take pictures of his private life. **As a result**, anyone who tries to invade his privacy is taken to court.

Brad Pitt doesn't let photographers take pictures of his private life.

... anyone who tries to invade his privacy is taken to court.

Class work

Linking word. ▸ WB, p. 70

Read the caption under the two pictures above.
Then read the phrases in A and B about film stars, and connect them with *As a result*.

A

1. People like to read about the private lives of famous actors.
2. People try to get close to or even touch celebrities.
3. Actors can't answer all the letters they are sent.
4. People love to see pictures of actors in their everyday lives.

B

1. ... actors sometimes have to be protected by bodyguards.
2. ... they have fan clubs.
3. ... celebrities are followed around by paparazzi.
4. ... many people buy magazines like *People Magazine*.

Role play.

Imagine you are one of the people you have just read about.
Follow your teacher's instructions.

What about you?

Answer the questions your teacher is going to ask about show business.

Discussion.

Do you agree or disagree?

Paparazzi go too far.

You have to look like a model to be a successful performer.

Personal expression

Get ready for a talk.

You are a lawyer.
You can choose to defend either Brad Pitt or a photographer he has taken to court.
Prepare your arguments.

Your teacher may record you.

Writing task.

You have just been offered a part in a film and you want to accept.
Your parents do not agree.
Imagine the conversation between you and them. ▸ WB, p. 71

Listening → Test

More about...

... Hollywood's landmarks ▸ WB, pp. 72-73

Hollywood is still the place to go to if you want to meet a film star or see a film being shot. Let's go on a tour of its legendary landmarks!

The giant Hollywood sign is 450 feet long and made up of 45 feet-high letters. It is perched on top of the highest hill in Los Angeles.

Originally, it said *Hollywoodland* and was an advertisement for a housing estate. But the last four letters were removed in 1945, after Hollywood had become the world's movie capital. The original sign used to have thousands of light bulbs which were checked daily.

Now, it is fenced in and an alarm system has been installed to prevent people from getting close to it and to avoid accidents. In the 1930s, a desperate actress killed herself by jumping off the giant letter H.

Grauman's Chinese Theater on Hollywood Boulevard is actually a cinema, but most people do not go there to watch a movie. They want to see where generations of film stars have left their footprints, handprints and autographs in wet cement.

New prints are constantly being added on the sidewalk in front of the theater. Tourists flock there to find their favourite actor's autograph or to compare their shoe sizes to the stars' footprints.

Some actors have left unique mementos of their own: John Wayne left an imprint of his fist, Groucho Marx of his cigar, and Whoopi Goldberg cut her hair and left an imprint of her locks!

If you want to see the places where your favourite movies were made, why not go on a guided tour of the studios? The most popular one is probably the **Universal Studios Tram Tour**.
There, you will be shown the sets where famous films were shot: *Back to the Future, Psycho, Charlie's Angels, Austin Powers 2* or *Apollo 13* ...

Every year in spring millions of people all over the world watch the **Academy Awards ceremony**.
The first Awards ceremony took place in 1929; films had just begun to talk and there were only 250 people present. In 1953, the Americans were able to watch it on television for the first time. Now, more than 3,000 people attend the ceremony.

Everyone is familiar with the suspense created by the system of nominations, the drama of the envelope being opened in public, and the famous phrase: "And the winner is ..."

The **Academy Awards statuette**, or Oscar, is awarded by the Academy of Motion Picture Arts and Sciences to the best professionals in a large number of categories, ranging from Best Leading Actor to Best Sound Editing.

Walt Disney holds the record of wins with 26 Academy Awards. He was presented with a full-size statuette and seven miniature ones for *Snow White and the Seven Dwarfs*! On the contrary, Alfred Hitchcock was nominated five times but never won any Academy Awards.

No one is sure how the statuette got its nickname. According to a popular story, the Academy librarian said it looked like her uncle Oscar, and the name stuck.

Remember and Practise

1 La voix passive

1. Un verbe au passif se forme ainsi :

auxiliaire *be* + participe passé du verbe

L'auxiliaire peut avoir toutes les formes.

Exemples :

The film ***is / was / is being / can be / must be / will be / has been*** */... shot in black and white.*

2. Pour parler d'un même fait, un locuteur peut mettre en relief différents éléments de la phrase.

Exemples :

• *Charles Addams* ***created*** *"The Addams Family".*

Ici, l'attention est focalisée sur la personne qui a fait l'action : créer les personnages de la famille Addams.

• *"The Addams Family"* ***was created*** *in 1937.*

L'attention est focalisée sur l'objet créé, sans en mentionner l'agent.

• *"The Addams Family"* ***was created by*** *C. Addams.*

Dans ce cas, l'attention est focalisée sur l'objet créé, et on y ajoute une information : par qui l'objet a été créé.

3. Quand l'agent est inconnu ou trop général, on ne le mentionne pas. En français, on utilise souvent dans ce cas le pronom « on ».

Exemple :

The scene was shot in a studio.
On a tourné la scène dans un studio.

A story that was adapted for the screen.

⚠ Réécris ces phrases en utilisant la voix passive, sans mentionner l'agent.

1. Someone found an old silent movie dating back from 1898.
2. They introduced sound in 1927.
3. They shoot most of the scenes in a studio.
4. They must invest big sums of money.
5. They will use a computer program.
6. Technicians have discovered a new way of colouring black and white films.
7. They are designing new special effects.

⚠ Construis des phrases complètes au présent ou au prétérit à la voix active ou à la voix passive. Utilise l'élément souligné comme sujet grammatical.

1. Nowadays / TV commercials / famous film directors. [often direct]
2. *The Birds* / Hitchcock / in 1963. [direct]
3. The violins / in the film *Psycho* / the heroine's screams. [evoke]
4. *Psycho* / horror movies. [influence]
5. Film stars / bodyguards. [often protect]
6. California's climate / film-makers. [attract]

2 Le style indirect: la concordance des temps

Lorsque le verbe introducteur est au passé *(said, asked, answered,* etc.), on décale le temps des verbes des paroles rapportées **vers le passé.**

Ce qui est au présent est rapporté au prétérit.

Exemples :

"You ***are*** *a fake!", she said.*
→ *She said (that) he* ***was*** *a fake.*

"I ***don't*** *trust you!", she said.*
→ *She said (that) she* ***didn't*** *trust him.*

"I ***can't*** *believe him!", she said.*
→ *She said (that) she* ***couldn't*** *believe him.*

"You are a fake!"
She said he was a fake.

▲ Rapporte chacune des phrases de ce dialogue au style indirect en utilisant les verbes introducteurs au prétérit (*said, asked, answered*).

Jane: I can meet your son at the airport. What time is he arriving?

Nicole: I don't know exactly. We have to check with the travel agency.

Jane: I'm not sure to recognize him. Can you send me his photo?

Nicole: That's a good idea.

3 La voix passive avec les verbes *ask, give* ...

1. Les verbes tels que *ask, show, tell, give, expect, teach, offer,* peuvent se construire avec **un complément d'attribution**.

Exemples :

They gave ***him*** *a present.*
Someone asked ***them*** *to come in.*

2. En anglais, contrairement au français, on peut utiliser ce **complément d'attribution** pour en faire le **sujet de la phrase au passif**.

Exemples :

He *was given a present.*
On lui a donné un cadeau.

They *were asked to come in.*
On leur a demandé d'entrer.

3. Comme pour toutes les phrases à la voix passive, le complément d'agent introduit par ***by*** n'est pas mentionné si celui-ci n'apporte pas d'information complémentaire.

When a secretary is asked to put money in a safe ...

▲ Réécris les phrases suivantes à la voix passive en prenant comme sujet le complément d'attribution (en italiques) et en ne mentionnant pas l'agent.

1. The witch offered *Snow White* a poisoned apple.
2. In an interview, a journalist asked *Hitchcock* why he made thrillers.
3. Hollywood awarded *Jodie Foster* several Oscars.
4. In this famous Drama School they will teach *you* how to act.
5. They have asked *him* to improvise a scene.
6. They expect *actors* to be able to use their imagination.
7. Before you start, they will send *you* a contract.
8. Someone told *me* that they needed extras.

4 Le gérondif après les prépositions

Toute préposition peut être suivie d'un nom (ou d'un groupe nominal), d'un pronom ou d'un verbe. Dans ce dernier cas, le verbe est au gérondif ou nom verbal.

Exemples :

You can get there ***by*** *bus.*
You can get there ***by*** *tak****ing*** *the ferry.*

I'm thinking ***of*** *an example.*
I'm thinking ***of*** *study****ing*** *abroad.*

I am not good ***at*** *maths.*
I am not good ***at*** *tell****ing*** *jokes.*

After *dinner they went to a pub.*
After *din****ing****, they went to a pub.*

Special effects are created by using tricks.

▲ Complète les phrases avec l'un des verbes suivants :

• *ask* • *be* • *cook* • *say* • *smoke* • *take* • *travel*

1. We learn a lot by ... .
2. I am afraid of ... questions.
3. I'm sorry for ... late.
4. He left without ... goodbye.
5. Are you good at ... ?
6. Most Americans have given up ...
7. How about ... a week's holiday?

Réutilise tes connaissances

▲1 Dis en anglais.

1. On m'a dit que vous tourniez un film.
2. On te demandera si tu sais chanter.
3. On nous a montré comment on crée des effets spéciaux.
4. J'ai peur de parler en public.
5. - Comment est-ce que je peux faire des progrès?
   - En t'entraînant tous les jours.

▲2 Comment peut-on traduire en français les consignes suivantes ?

1. [*A l'entrée d'une cathédrale*]
   VISITORS ARE ASKED TO CONDUCT THEMSELVES QUIETLY IN THE CATHEDRAL
2. [*Dans un hôtel*]
   CUSTOMERS ARE REQUESTED TO LEAVE THEIR VALUABLES AT THE DESK
3. [*A un guichet de retrait automatique d'argent*]
   YOUR TRANSACTION IS BEING PROCESSED

5 Welcome to the United Kingdom!

Objectifs

1— Le conditionnel
If your teacher organized an exchange ...
Le style indirect : *wonder*

2— L'expression de la préférence
What would you rather do?

3— Les composés en *WH-ever*
Whoever studies English should visit Britain.

Roman Britain

From 55 BC onwards
The Romans conquered Britain and settled nearly as far north as what is now the Scottish border. There, they built a wall (Hadrian's Wall) against the invaders from the North. They also built roads and cities (London, Bath, York, ...).
After the Romans left, the Angles, the Saxons and the Vikings invaded the country.

The Normans

1066
William, Duke of Normandy, defeated the Saxon king, Harold, at the battle of Hastings.
William the Conqueror became King of England.
Many French words were introduced into the English language.

How much do you know about the United Kingdom?

QUIZ

Look at the map and read the information.
Then do the quiz in your workbook. ▶ **WB, p. 74**

Great Britain: England, Scotland and Wales
population of Great Britain: 60 million inhabitants
United Kingdom : Great Britain and Northern Ireland
flag of the United Kingdom: "The Union Jack"

The Tudors

1485-1603
Henry VIII (reign: 1509-1547) broke from the Catholic Church and proclaimed himself Head of the Church of England.
He had six wives and ordered two of them to be executed.
His daughter, Elizabeth I (reign: 1558-1603), encouraged the arts – it was the time of Shakespeare – and also English sailors and traders to settle abroad and to create colonies.

The Stuarts

1603-1714
Charles I was executed in 1649 after the English Civil War (1642-1645). Britain became a Republic and for eleven years, Oliver Cromwell was its Lord Protector. But in 1660 the monarchy was restored when Charles II became king.

1666
The Great Fire destroyed most of the city of London, but few people were killed.

The Victorian Age

1837-1901
Victoria became Queen of Great Britain and Ireland at the age of eighteen and Empress of India in 1876.
During her long reign the British Empire was the greatest world power thanks to its industries, its banking system and also its colonies in Africa, India, Canada, Australia and New Zealand.

The 20th century

1921
Ireland became independent.

WWII
Britain played a major role during the war with Winston Churchill as Prime Minister.

After WWII
Britain lost its colonial empire but maintained cultural ties with its former colonies through the Commonwealth.

1 If your teacher organized an exchange ...

1. Listen and answer. ▸ WB, p. 76

Listen to six sentences and answer, using one of the following phrases:

Yes, please! / No, thank you.

Yes, I would. / No, I wouldn't.

I'd love to! / I'd hate it!

2. A quiz. ▸ WB, pp. 76-77

If your teacher organized an exchange with a class in Great Britain, how would you react in the following situations?
Read and tick the answers in your workbook.

1. If it rained all the time during your trip, ...
- a you would keep moaning.
- b you wouldn't mind.
- c you would sing in the rain.

2. If you were offered a strange-looking dessert, ...
- a you wouldn't dare to refuse.
- b you would pretend to be full.
- c you would ask for the recipe.

3. If you were very tired, ...
- a you would pretend to be ill.
- b you wouldn't complain.
- c you would ask for permission to stay at your partner's home.

4. If you didn't have any pocket-money left, ...
- a you would borrow some from your host family.
- b you wouldn't buy any souvenirs.
- c you would ask your teacher to lend you some.

5. If you got lost, ...
- a you wouldn't know what to do.
- b you would call your parents on a mobile.
- c you would stay where you are and wait for the teacher.

6. If you didn't get on with your exchange partner, ...
- a you would complain to your teacher.
- b you would try to be friendly all the same.
- c you would ignore your partner and go out with your friends.

7. If you didn't understand what people are saying, ...
- a you wouldn't speak at all.
- b you would ask them to repeat.
- c you would keep answering "Yes!" all the time.

8. If you broke a vase in your exchange partner's house, ...
- a you would apologize.
- b you would offer to pay for another one.
- c you would try to hide the broken pieces.

3. Group work. ▸ WB, p. 78

Now, make dialogues as in these two examples:

A. *What **would** you **do** if you got lost?*
B. *If I got lost, I **would call** my parents on a mobile. What about you?*
A. *So **would I**. / I **wouldn't!***

A. *What **would** you **do** if you were very tired?*
B. *If I were very tired, I **wouldn't complain**. What about you?*
A. *Neither **would I**! / I **would** !*

4. Listen and make comments. ▸ WB, p. 79

Imagine your parents moved to England.
Say what you *would* or *wouldn't* ***have to*** *do*, and what you *wouldn't* ***be able to*** *do*.

5. Reported speech. ▸ WB, p. 79

Mrs Dawson has organized an exchange with a French class. Today, Kevin, one of the students, is missing. She is very worried.

Read what is going on in her mind.

Then make comments as in this example:

*The teacher **wonders** where Kevin **can** be.*

Now, Kevin has found his group again. His teacher is telling him that she was very worried.

Report what she tells him, as in this example:

*We **were** all **wondering** where you **could** be.*

Listening

1. Listening comprehension.

Listen to the conversation and do the task in your workbook. ▸ WB, pp. 80-81

2. Summary.

Now, sum up the story with the help in your workbook. ▸ WB, p. 81

Oral practice

Les premières syllabes *a-* ou *be-*

■ Ecoute et repère les syllabes accentuées dans les mots suivants :

• *abroad* • *alone* • *above* • *again*
• *agree* • *apologize*

• *before* • *between* • *behind* • *because*

■ Fais l'exercice d'entraînement dans ton *workbook*. ▸ WB, p. 80

2 What would you rather do?

1. Pair work. ▸ WB, p. 82

Work with a partner and ask each other questions as in this example:

A: *If you went to London, what **would** you **rather** do: watch a football match at Wembley or a tennis match at Wimbledon?*

B: *I'**d rather** watch a tennis match at Wimbledon.*

Now look at the pictures and make more dialogues.

CAMBRIDGE

[go rowing] on the river Cam

[visit] a college

SCOTLAND

[watch] the Highlands Games

[visit] a castle

BRIGHTON

[play games] on the Pier

[visit] the Royal Pavilion

LONDON

[go shopping] in Camden Street

[go shopping] in Oxford Street

2. Listen and speak. ▸ WB, p. 82

Listen to the questions and say what choice you would make, using: *I'd rather ... than ...*

Listening

1. Listening comprehension.

Listen to the conversation
and do the task in your workbook. ▸ **WB, p. 83**

2. Summary.

Now, sum up the story
with the help in your workbook. ▸ **WB, p. 83**

Oral practice

L'accent secondaire

■ Un mot de plusieurs syllabes peut être accentué :

• sur la première syllabe :

Exemples :
borrow • *recipe* • *dictionary*

• sur la deuxième syllabe :

Exemples :
complain • *another*• *apologize*

• à partir d'une accentuation sur la troisième syllabe, on ajoute un autre accent, dit secondaire, deux syllabes avant l'accent principal.

Exemples :
po/pu/LA/tion • *e/co/NO/mic*

Dans les transcriptions phonétiques, l'accent principal est noté ainsi : [ˈ] et l'accent secondaire ainsi : [ˌ]

Exemples : [ˌpɒpjʊˈleɪʃən] [ˌiːkəˈnɒmɪk]

■ Ecoute et répète les mots suivants en repérant les accents principaux et secondaires.

- *introduce*
- *conversation*
- *independent*
- *unemployment*
- *international*
- *accommodation*

■ Fais l'exercice d'entraînement dans ton *workbook*. ▸ **WB, p. 82**

3 Whoever studies English should visit Britain.

Wherever you are, you're never far from a pub.

Whoever goes to England should try a cream tea.

Whatever you're looking for can be found at Harrod's.

Whenever someone wants to express his opinion in public, he can go to Speakers' Corner in Hyde Park.

1. Listen and speak. ▸ WB, p. 84

• *everyone who*	→	*whoever*	• *everywhere*	→	*wherever*
• *everything*	→	*whatever*	• *every time*	→	*whenever*

Using the chart above, transform the sentences you hear as in this example:

You hear: ***Everywhere** you go in Britain, you can find an Indian restaurant.*
You say: ***Wherever** you go in Britain, you can find an Indian restaurant.*

2. What about you? ▸ WB, p. 84

What can you say about your own life? Complete the following sentences:

Whenever I get a good mark, … *Whenever I get home late, …*
Whenever I feel depressed, … *Whenever I have a test, …*

3. Listening comprehension. → Test

CLOTHES ▸ WB, p. 80

stylish / classy ['staɪlɪʃ]	*élégant*
trendy	*à la mode, «tendance»*
out of fashion	*démodé*
fashionable	*à la mode*
naff	*«moche»*
casual ['kæʒjʊl]	*décontracté*
formal dress	*tenue habillée*
tight [taɪt]	*serré*
tight-fitting	*moulant*
loose [lʊːs]	*ample, pas serré*
wool / woolen [wʊːl] / ['wʊːlən]	*laine / en laine*
cotton	*coton / en coton*
leather ['leðə]	*cuir / en cuir*
silk	*soie / en soie*
It suits [suːts] **me.**	*Cela me va bien. (C'est mon style.)*
It fits me.	*Cela me va bien. (C'est ma taille.)*
What size are you?	*Quelle est votre taille?*
S/he is dressed to kill.	*Il / Elle est sur son «trente-et-un».*

1. Listen and repeat.
Listen and repeat the words from the list.

2. Listen and answer.
Listen to the questions and give the right answer.

3. A hidden message.

ðiːz dʒiːns dəʊnt suːt juː

Coin New Words

You can coin new words by combining two nouns, as in these examples:

a **fashion designer**	a **flea market**	a **haircut**
a **handbag**	an **earring**	a **name brand**

Now, do the exercise in your workbook. ▸ WB, p. 86

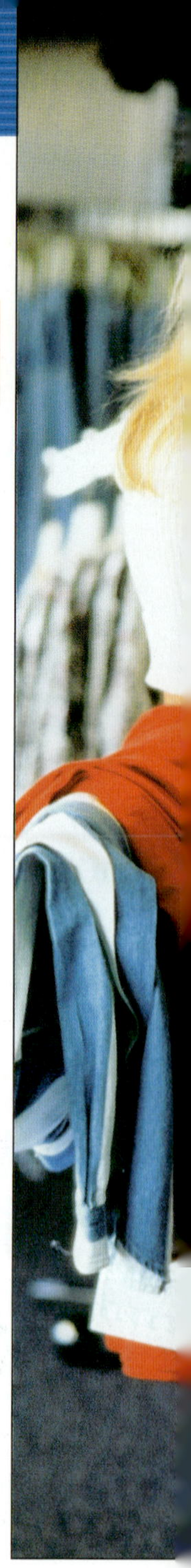

THE BRITISH AND FASHION

Eccentric ways of dressing are not an uncommon sight in the streets of London. No wonder English fashion designers take their inspiration from people in the street. Listen to Helen and to Paul. ▸ **WB, pp. 87-88**

For me, fashion is fun. On Friday nights, out goes the school uniform and in comes whatever I'm in the mood for. It all depends on where I go and who I'm with. I can be two or three different "me's" in one weekend!

My parents and I never agree about what suits me and what doesn't, but they don't make too many comments **as long as** I buy my clothes with my own pocket-money.

What I love about fashion is that I can let my imagination go. I can experiment with colours, shapes and designs **as long as** I don't have to spend loads of money, of course. Actually, whenever I get a chance, I go to flea markets to buy second-hand things that add an artistic touch. I refuse to wear brand name clothes! They're worse than uniforms, everyone looks the same. Plus, they're super expensive. And I'd rather not look like a billboard, anyway!

Helen, 15

Wherever you go in London you'll see young people dressed in unusual clothes. If this were another country, people would turn their heads in surprise – or shock! But we English don't stare at each other in public. So young people here feel free to express themselves through their clothes. But the problem is, how do you manage to get noticed if nobody looks at you? Well, you do whatever you can to attract people's attention.

Looking different is also young people's way of rebelling. It's their way of saying, "I don't want to be like you". But as you get older, you get over it. I remember the fuss my own parents made over my haircut when I was 15, and look at me now ...

Paul, 28

as long as...

I can experiment with colours, shapes and designs ...

I don't have to spend loads of money.

Class work

Linking word. ▸ WB, p. 88

Read the caption under the two pictures above. Then read the phrases in A and B about Great Britain, and connect them with *as long as*.

A

1. You'll enjoy visiting the Tower of London ...
2. A visit to Tate Modern is a must ...
3. You'll find Indian meals delicious ...
4. The view from the London Eye is fantastic ...

B

1. ... you're interested in modern art.
2. ... it is not a cloudy day.
3. ... you don't mind queueing.
4. ... you like spicy food.

Role play.

Imagine you are one of the people you have just read about. Follow your teacher's instructions.

What about you?

Answer the questions you teacher is going to ask about fashion.

Discussion.

Do you agree or disagree?

Looking different is also young people's way of rebelling.

Brand names are worse than uniforms.

Personal expression

Get ready for a talk.

Do you think that clothes reveal someone's personality and interests?

Your teacher may record you.

Writing task.

Imagine an argument between a teenager and his / her parents about the way s/he is dressed. ▸ WB, p. 89

Listening
→ Test

... PLACES WORTH VISITING ALONG THE RIVER THAMES ▸ WB, pp. 90-9

The river Thames is England's longest river flowing through southern England and connecting London with the sea.

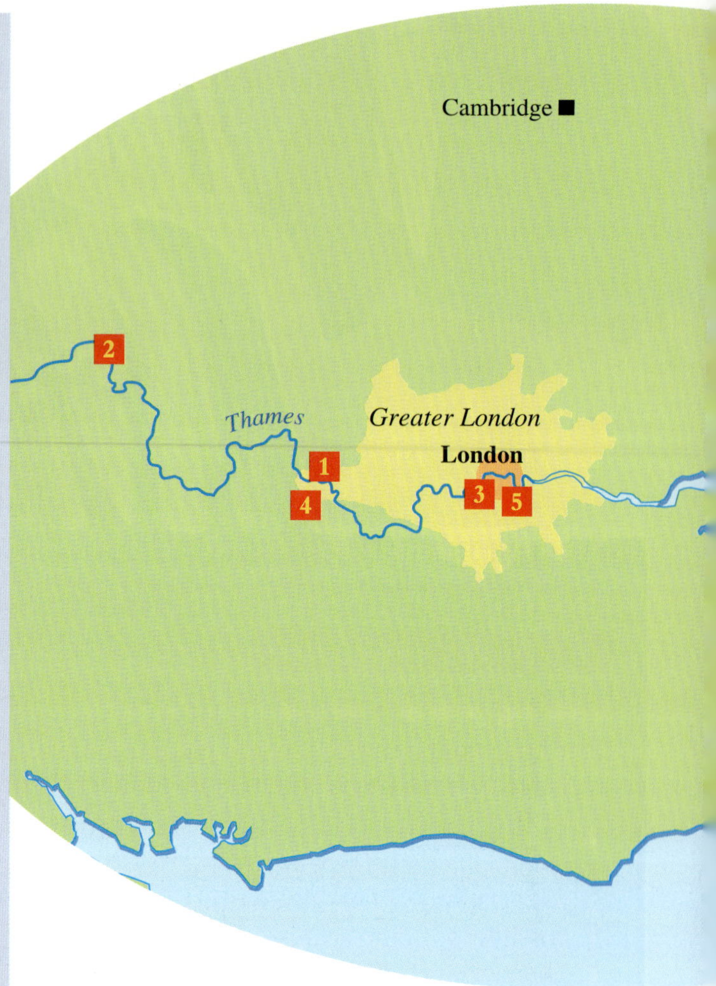

1 Eton

Eton College is one of the most famous "public" schools in England. It was founded in 1440 by King Henry IV and was originally designed to provide free education to poor students. But since the 19th century, it has been one of the most exclusive schools in the world: only the wealthiest families can afford fees of over 31,000 euros a year.
There are about 1,300 boys, aged thirteen to eighteen, all boarders, admitted after a very competitive exam. Results are excellent and discipline is very strict. Many members of the Royal Family have been educated there and Eton has produced eighteen Prime Ministers.

2 Oxford

Oxford university is one of the oldest and most prestigious universities in the world. It is made up of 36 colleges which were founded between the 13th and the 16th centuries. Cambridge University was founded at approximately the same period.
To get into Oxford or Cambridge, students have to get excellent results at their A levels (the equivalent of the *baccalauréat*).
Many different subjects are taught there (sciences, medicine, law, liberal arts – philosophy, literature, ... – maths, computer science ...) in ideal conditions (very small groups of students).
Both universities – often referred to as *Oxbridge* – compete every year in a boat race on the River Thames, a very popular sporting event broadcast on TV.

3 The Globe Theatre in London

The original Globe, built of wood and covered with thatch was destroyed by fire. This is where *Romeo and Juliet, Hamlet, Macbeth* and many other plays were shown for the first time (with male actors only!).

In the 16th century, theatre was very popular and people from all classes of society went to see plays. The cheapest way was to stand in the middle, in front of the stage, where there was no roof. (You just had to hope it didn't rain!) There was no lighting and plays were only performed during the summer and in daylight. The audience was very noisy and responsive. They often addressed the actors and if they didn't like the play, they threw things at them.

A faithful reproduction of Shakespeare's theatre was built in the 1990s.

4 Windsor

Windsor castle is one of the seven official Royal residences. You can visit the State Apartments– which contain a vast collection of paintings–but not the private apartments, of course! You can also visit St George's Chapel where many Royals are buried. In 1992 a fire destroyed parts of the castle but it has now been restored.

The Royals who employ about 700 people to maintain all these residences, receive a Civil List–a sort of annual salary to pay their employees' wages, and to cover their personal and official expenses.

5 Greenwich

This pleasant area on the south bank of the Thames is intimately connected with British sea-power: near the pier is the famous *Cutty Sark*, a clipper (sailing ship) that was used to transport tea and spices from China.

But of course Greenwich is best known for the zero meridian, materialized by a brass strip in the garden of the Old Royal Observatory, which gives the official GMT time to the whole world.

Remember and Practise

1 Le conditionnel

1. Formation : *would* + base verbale

Exemple:

*What **would** you **like** to visit in London?*

2. Pour faire **une hypothèse**, exprimer une situation imaginaire, on emploie ***if*** suivi d'un **verbe au prétérit**. Ce « prétérit modal » ne fait pas référence à un événement passé : il exprime une éventualité et non une réalité. Pour le verbe ***be***, on emploie ***were*** à toutes les personnes.

Exemples:

*If I **were** rich ...*

*If I **won** in the Lottery ...*

• Pour exprimer le **résultat** consécutif à une hypothèse (ce qui arriverait si ...), on emploie le conditionnel.

Exemple:

hypothèse	**résultat**
If I won in the Lottery ... Si je gagnais au Loto ...	*I **would** travel.* je voyagerais.

• Pour exprimer ce que l'on **pourrait** ou **devrait** faire, on emploie les équivalents des modaux.

Exemples:

*can → **would / wouldn't be able to***

*I **wouldn't be able to** see my friends any more.*
Je ne pourrais plus voir mes amis.

*must → **would / wouldn't have to***

*I **would have to** speak English all the time.*
Je devrais parler anglais tout le temps.

If your teacher organized an exchange ...

1 Utilise les verbes entre crochets pour construire des phrases complètes.

1. If you [find] a large sum of money in the street, what you [do]?
2. Tourists [stay] longer if hotels [be] less expensive.
3. If Alex [not keep moaning] all the time, he [be] more pleasant to travel with.
4. I'm sure Sue [be] happy if you [call] her.
5. Do you think you [feel] miserable if your parents [have] to move abroad?

2 Imagine ce que tu devrais faire ou ne pourrais plus faire dans les situations suivantes:

1. If I didn't have any pocket-money, ...
2. If I didn't have any friends, ...
3. If I went to live abroad, ...
4. If I couldn't speak English at all, ...

3 Construis des phrases complètes avec les éléments suivants :

1. If / him / call / be able to / phone number / I / his / I / would / knew
2. went / a ride / If / on / London / I / I / would / to / the London Eye / have
3. it / a trip / love / my class / organized / with / I / was / would / abroad / If

2 Le style indirect : *wonder*

• Le verbe ***wonder*** introduit au style indirect une **question** que l'on se pose **à soi-même**.

Exemple:

*She **wonders** where Kevin can be.*
Elle se demande où Kevin peut bien être.

• La construction après *wonder* est celle des questions indirectes :

***wonder** wh- / if* + sujet + verbe

Exemples:

She wonders, "Where is Kevin? Is he all right?"
→ She wonders where Kevin is.
→ She wonders if he is all right.

• Selon le temps du verbe introducteur, on applique la concordance des temps.

Exemples:

*She **wonders** if he **has** her phone number.*

*She **was wondering** if he **had** her phone number.*

She wonders where Kevin can be.

Complète chaque phrase ci-dessous.

1. "How long will we have to wait?"
   They wonder ...
2. "What does it taste like?"
   He wonders ...
3. "Do we have to bring a present?"
   They were wondering ...
4. "When can we give a party?"
   We were wondering ...

3 L'expression de la préférence

• L'expression ***I'd rather ...*** *(I would rather ...)* s'emploie pour exprimer une préférence dans une situation où l'on doit faire un choix.

Exemple:

*I **would rather** go (I'**d rather** go) and see a match.*
Je préférerais / j'aimerais mieux aller voir un match.

C'est généralement la forme contractée de l'auxiliaire *would* qui est employée (*'d*).

• Lorsque l'on mentionne le deuxième élément du choix, on l'introduit par ***than***.

Exemple:

*I'd rather eat out **than** (eat) at home.*

Je préférerais manger au restaurant plutôt qu'à la maison.

What would you rather do?

▲ **Si on te donnait à choisir entre ces diverses propositions, quelles seraient tes préférences?**

1. live in Britain / in the United States
2. be an actor or an actress / a singer
3. visit Scotland / Ireland
4. have longer winter holidays / longer summer holidays
5. win a trip in a space shuttle / a trip to Australia

4 Les composés en *WH-ever*

Pour exprimer l'idée que quelque chose est vrai quels que soient la personne, l'endroit, le moment, l'objet ou l'action envisagés, on utilise les composés en *WH-ever, "ever"* traduisant une généralisation.

Exemples:

***Whenever** I go to England, I take the Eurostar.*
Chaque fois que je vais en Angleterre, je prends l'Eurostar.

***Wherever** I go, I try to find a pub where I can have a meal.*
Quel que soit l'endroit où je vais, j'essaie de trouver un pub pour y prendre un repas.

***Whoever** likes city life loves London.*
Toute personne qui aime la vie dans une grande ville adore Londres.

***Whatever** you're wearing, no one will notice you.*
Quel que soit ce que vous portez, personne ne vous remarquera.

Whoever studies English should visit Britain.

▲1 **Transforme les phrases suivantes en substituant les expressions soulignées par un mot en *WH-ever*.**

1. Every time there is a Royal wedding or a funeral, the ceremony is broadcast on television all over the world.
2. Everything that is in Buckingham Palace belongs to the Royal family.
3. Everyone who likes gardening will love English gardens.
4. In spring time every place you go in Britain, you see daffodils.

▲2 **Complète les phrases suivantes par un mot en *WH-ever*.**

1. ... he says is funny.
2. ... I go to England, I buy different kinds of tea.
3. ... is interested in history will enjoy the numerous museums in Britain.
4. ... the English established colonies, English became one of the official languages.

Réutilise tes connaissances

▲1 **Dis en anglais.**

1. Si j'étais toi, je m'excuserais.
2. J'aimerais mieux emprunter de l'argent à mon professeur qu'à ma famille hôtesse.
3. Je me demande pourquoi il se plaint.
4. Quoi que je dise, tu n'es jamais d'accord.

▲2 **Complète les phrases suivantes.**

1. I'd rather .... than work in an office.
2. Whoever ... will be punished.
3. If I were an adult, I would have to ...
4. If I were an adult, I would be able to ...

6 Australia, a country and a continent

Objectifs

1— Le double comparatif
More and more changes are taking place in Australia.
Le style indirect :
le passage de *will* à *would*

2— Le *present perfect* avec *be + -ing*
What have they been doing?

3— Le *present perfect* avec *be + -ing*
for ... / since ...
He's been driving for 7 hours.

The native Australians

50,000 BC
Nomads arrived on the continent, probably coming from Indonesia. Their descendants, the Aborigines, have tried to preserve their culture throughout the centuries.

The European settlers

The early 1600s
Discovery of the western coast by Dutch then by Portuguese explorers.

1770
Captain Cook, an English officer, discovered New Zealand and the eastern coast of Australia.

The convicts

1788
Foundation of the British colony of New South Wales.
Britain started to transport prisoners to Australia. They constructed roads or worked on the lands given to the British soldiers and officers.
In all, 168,000 prisoners were shipped to Australia until transportation was abolished in 1868.

How much do you know about Australia?

QUIZ

Look at the maps and read the information.
Then do the quiz in your workbook ▸ **WB, p. 92**

population: 19 million inhabitants
surface area: about as large as the United States
desert land: 30% of Australia
the Outback: 80% of Australia
currency: the Australian dollar

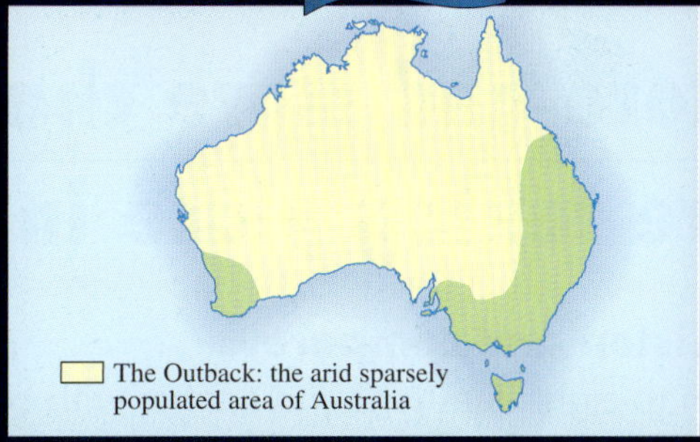

The gold diggers

The 1850s
Gold was discovered and the number of free settlers greatly increased.
They were not only from Ireland and England, but also from the rest of Europe, America and China.
Few of them actually made fortunes from gold, and many settled as farmers or shopkeepers.

A new nation

1901
Australia became an independent nation composed of six states and two territories.
It maintained legal and cultural ties with Great Britain through the Commonwealth.

The new "Aussies"

After WWII
An immigration programme whose slogan was "Populate or Perish" was set up to increase Australia's population. During the last fifty years more than a million non-British European immigrants and a large number of Vietnamese refugees as well as other Asians have come to live in Australia.

The Aboriginal citizens

1962
The Aborigines were finally recognized as full Australian citizens.

2000
The Aboriginal athlete Cathy Freeman was chosen to light the flame for the opening of the Olympic Games in Sydney.

Basics

1 More and more changes are taking place in Australia.

Review

1. Listen and compare.

Listen to eight questions and answer with complete sentences. ▸ **WB, p. 94**

2. Make comments. ▸ WB, p. 95

Use the information below to make comments, as in these examples:

The percentage of ...
- exports to Asia ↑ — *The percentage of exports to Asia **is increasing**.*
- exports to Great Britain ↓ — *The percentage of exports to Great Britain **is decreasing**.*

The number of ...
- kangaroos ↑
- sheep ↓
- koalas ↓

The amount of ...
- imported wine ↓
- Australian wine ↑

The number of students learning ...
- French ↓
- an Asian language ↑

Immigration from ...
- Great Britain ↓
- Asia ↑

3. Draw conclusions. ▸ WB, p. 95

Now, draw conclusions. Begin your sentences as in these examples:

*There are **more and more** kangaroos.* ↑ ↑ *There are **fewer and fewer** koalas.* ↓ ↓
*There is **more and more** ...* ↑ ↑ *There is **less and less** ...* ↓ ↓

*Surfing is getting **more and more** popular.*

*Australians use sun protection because they are getting **better and better** informed about the dangers of the sun.*

4. Make comments. ▸ WB, p. 96

Use the information in the boxes to comment about the changes that are taking place in Australia, as in the example under each picture:

- *surfing*
- *Australians*
- *farms*
- *the influence of Asia*
- *the influence of Great-Britain*
- *flights to Australia*
- *Australian students*
- *the effects of global warming*
- *coastal cities*

- *weak*
- *populated*
- *cheap*
- *popular*
- *bad*
- *big*
- *well informed ...*
- *good at Japanese*
- *strong*

5. Listen.

Listen and choose the right answer. ▸ WB, p. 96

6. Reported speech.

Look at the pictures on page 84 and read what the wine-grower said.

*In the next few years, more and more restaurants **will** serve Australian wine.*

*The wine-grower **said** that in the next few years, more and more restaurants **would** serve Australian wine.*

Report what the student said as in the example above.
Then do the exercise in your workbook. ▸ WB, pp. 96-97

Listening

1. Listening comprehension.

Listen to the conversation and do the task in your workbook.
▸ WB, pp. 97-98

2. Summary.

Now, sum up the story with the help in your workbook. ▸ WB, p. 98

Oral practice

L'accent de mot : le rôle des terminaisons en voyelles doubles ou en -ese

■ Ecoute et repère les syllabes accentuées dans les mots suivants :

- *kangaroo*
- *monsoon*
- *engineer*
- *refugee*
- *career*
- *Japanese*
- *Chinese*
- *Vietnamese*
- *Portuguese*

Quelle règle peux-tu tirer ?

■ Fais l'exercice d'entraînement dans ton *workbook*. ▸ WB, p. 97

2 What have they been doing?

- *full*
- *clean*
- *flooded*
- *exhausted*
- *wet*
- *sun-tanned*
- *dusty*
- *furious*

1. Make comments. ▸ WB, pp. 99-100

Each picture shows the result of an activity that has been taking place. First, make comments about the present results, using the adjectives in the box, as in this example:

The road is flooded.

Now give an explanation with the help of the films below, as in this example:

*The road is flooded because it **has been** rain**ing** a lot.*

[rain a lot]

[a dingo ... attack the sheep]

[work a lot]

[lie in the sun]

[volunteers ... collect tin]

[surf]

[the tourists ... drive through the desert]

[eat eucalyptus leaves]

2. Listen.

Listen to the recording and do the task in your workbook. ▸ WB, p. 100

3. Classwork. ▸ WB, p. 100

Say one of the sentences in the green box to one of your classmates. S/he will have to give you an explanation using one of the verbs given in the yellow box, as in this example:

A: *You're out of breath!*

B: *Well, yes, I've been running / jogging...*

- *You're out of breath!*
- *You have such a nice tan!*
- *You have lost your voice!*
- *Your eyes are red!*
- *You've got grease on your hands!*
- *You've got a stain on your T-shirt!*
- *You look exhausted! You have bags under your eyes!*

- *run*
- *jog*
- *repair*
- *cook*
- *sing*
- *shout*
- *study*
- *lie*
- *sun-bathe*
- *cry*

Listening

1. Listening comprehension.

Listen to the conversation and do the task in your workbook.
▸ WB, pp. 100-101

2. Summary.

Now, sum up the story with the help in your workbook. ▸ WB, p. 101

Oral practice

Les auxiliaires accentués

■ Pour insister sur le fait que ce que l'on dit est vrai, on accentue l'auxiliaire du groupe verbal en utilisant la forme d'insistance:
It is hot! (Il fait vraiment chaud !)
par opposition à la forme neutre:
It's hot. (Il fait chaud.)

■ Lorsque la forme verbale n'a pas d'auxiliaire apparent, comme la forme affirmative du présent et du prétérit simples:
You look exhausted.
(Tu as l'air épuisé.)
cet auxiliaire réapparaît à la forme d'insistance:
You do look exhausted.
(Tu as vraiment l'air épuisé.)

■ Cet auxiliaire a alors plusieurs caractéristiques qui distinguent l'énoncé d'un énoncé neutre:
- il est toujours en forme pleine (jamais contractée);
- à l'oral, il est prononcé avec une chute intonative (le point de départ de l'auxiliaire est aigu et glisse vers un registre grave);
- à l'écrit, on signale cette forme d'insistance en soulignant l'auxiliaire ou en utilisant des italiques.

■ Fais l'exercice d'entraînement dans ton *workbook*. ▸ WB, p. 100

Review

3 He's been driving for 7 hours.

1. Listen. ▸ WB, p. 102

Listen to the recording and complete each sentence with *since ...* or *for ...*

2. What about you? ▸ WB, p. 102

Ask your classmates how long they have been living in ... (a place); playing / doing ... (a sport); studying ...; collecting ... ; learning how to play... (a musical instrument).

*How long **have** you **been** study**ing** English?*

*I've **been** study**ing** English **for** five years, **since** I was nine.*

3. Pairwork. ▸ WB, pp. 103-104

Look at the pictures and, using the expressions given below, make dialogues as in this example:

A: *How long has Joe been driving his "road train"?*
B: *He has been driving his "road train" **for** 7 hours.*

a "road train"

- Joe [drive] his "road train"... 7 hours.
- The farmers [gather] cattle on a farm ... this morning.
- The passengers [travel] on the Indian Pacific ... 30 hours.
- The safari lover [drive] through the Outback ... he left Perth.
- The students [visit] Sydney ... 3 days.
- The divers [film] a coral reef ... 11 a.m.

4. Listening comprehension. → Test

cattle on a farm

the Indian Pacific

the Outback

Sydney

a coral reef

More Words

NATURE ▸ WB, p. 105

leaf / leaves	*feuille (s)*
trunk	*tronc*
branch	*branche*
grass	*herbe*
bush	*brousse*
rainforest	*forêt tropicale*
dry/ wet season	*saison sèche / humide*
hurricane ['hʌrɪkən]	*ouragan*
typhoon [taɪ'fuːn]	*typhon*
flooded ['flʌdɪd]	*inondé*
bushfire	*feu de brousse*
drought [draʊt]	*sécheresse*

ANIMALS ▸ WB, p. 105

reptile ['reptaɪl]	*reptile*
mammal ['mæməl]	*mammifère*
shark	*requin*
dolphin ['dɒlfɪn]	*dauphin*
whale [weɪl]	*baleine*
viper ['vaɪpə]	*vipère*
ant	*fourmi*
mosquito	*moustique*
wasp	*guêpe*
bee	*abeille*
fly [flaɪ]	*mouche*
flea [fliː]	*puce*

1. Listen and repeat.

Listen and repeat the words from the list.

2. Listen and answer.

Listen to the questions and give the right answer.

3. A hidden message.

ðeɪ həʊpt ðeə wʊd biː 'fjuːə ən 'fjuːə bʊʃfaɪəz ɪn ðə fjuːtʃə

Coin New Words

You can coin new words by combining a verb and a noun, as in these examples:

a driving licence
a bathing suit
a boarding school
a fishing rod

Now, do the exercise in your workbook. ▸ WB, p. 105

Growing up in the Outback

Jane Parris, 15, has been studying in a boarding school in Sydney for three years. She is talking about her life in the Outback where she spent her childhood. ▸ **WB, pp. 106-107**

1. Why are you studying in a boarding school?

Like many students whose parents are farmers, I didn't really have a choice. We live in the Outback, and the nearest town, Alice Springs, is 160 miles away. That is why, up until the age of 12, I studied at home in what is called “School of the Air”.

2. Can you tell us about it?

Well, basically, it's a school where you work at home – with 30-minute lessons on the "radio" every morning, plus a 10-minute one-to-one lesson with a teacher once a week. I used to spend about five hours a day working on my lessons, like any other student in a regular school. I sent the teachers my homework, they marked it and sent it back with their comments.

3. Was it difficult for you to adapt to a regular school?

Well, I used to study alone and do my homework at my own pace. So, the first time I was told that I had only one hour to do an essay, I panicked! I had to learn more and more quickly, and also to wait for my turn to answer questions in class. It was a little bit difficult for me to realize that I wasn't the only one the teacher listened to!

4. Do you mean that until the age of 12 you didn't have any classmates?

That's right – actually, my best friends were my brothers. I learned to play rugby with them **even though** there were only four of us! I didn't do any team sport until I came to boarding school.

5. What's it like living in the Outback?

As a kid I used to love it. And I think it's great to live so close to nature. I got to know which animals are dangerous like reptiles, spiders, ants, and which ones aren't, which plants are poisonous and which ones aren't. I don't panic when I see a bushfire, I don't run away when I see a snake.

Plus, I know how to drive a tractor, and even co-pilot a helicopter!

6. How do you communicate with the outside world?

We use the Internet and it's easier and easier to communicate. So you see, **even though** we're isolated, we're in contact with people from everywhere.

... we're isolated, we're in contact with people from everywhere.

Class work

Linking word. ▸ WB, p. 108

Read the caption under the two pictures above.
Then read the phrases in A and B about the Outback, and connect them with *Even though*.

A

1. ... the Outback is hot and dusty,
2. ... there are no schools,
3. ... the desert occupies a large part of the Outback,
4. ... some animals there look harmless,

B

1. children can have an education.
2. they have deadly poison in their skin.
3. many tourists drive and even hike through it.
4. some areas are covered with savannah or rainforest.

Role play.

Imagine you are one of the people you have just read about. Follow your teacher's instructions.

What about you?

Answer the questions your teacher is going to ask about living in an isolated place.

Discussion.

Do you agree or disagree?

It's getting easier and easier to communicate.

It's great to live so close to nature!

Personal expression

Get ready for a talk.

Compare your childhood with Jane's. How different is it? Does her childhood in the Outback make you dream?

Your teacher may record you.

Writing task.

A young student who used to live in the Outback has just moved to Sydney. S/he writes to friends to tell them how different life is in the city. ▸ WB, p. 109

Listening
→ Test

More about...

... THE ABORIGINES OF AUSTRALIA ▸ WB, pp. 110-111

The word "Aborigine" means "from the beginning". This is the name that the native Australians were given by the Europeans; but they prefer to call themselves "Kooris". Their culture and languages are the oldest in the world.

First contact with the British colonists

In the 18th century, when the first British settlers arrived in Australia, there were about 300,000 Aborigines who were living in different nomadic tribes and spoke more than 300 different languages. The British colonists declared that the continent was *terra nullius* (= uninhabited by humans). More and more white settlers occupied the fertile land and pushed the Aborigines further and further away into the arid areas of the Outback.

The Aborigines were even hunted like animals and some of their sacred sites were destroyed.

Their population decreased dramatically. Many died from the diseases brought by the white settlers. In 1900 only 67,000 Aborigines had survived.

From second-class to fully recognized citizens

Until the second half of the 20th century, the Aborigines were considered as second class citizens: they were not included in the census, and they didn't get the right to vote until 1967.

Today there are about 380,000 Aborigines. But their levels of education, health, employment and their life expectancy are much lower than the other Australians. They also have the nation's highest rates of imprisonment, alcoholism and drug abuse.

In 1992 the Australian government officially recognized that the policy of *terra nullius* was not valid, that the Aborigines were the first human occupants of Australia. As a result, some lands have been returned to the Aborigines, their traditional owners.

Uluru (Ayers Rock)
Uluru is the Aboriginal name of a monolith which is also called "Ayers Rock". It is situated in the Outback, not very far from Alice Springs. It's an extremely popular site which is visited by thousands of tourists every year. It is especially impressive at sunset when the red rock spectacularly changes colour.

This site belongs to an Aboriginal community and it is considered sacred. The Aboriginal owners prefer visitors not to climb the rock and more and more tourists now respect their wishes and take the walks around the base of the rock.

Aboriginal art, a sacred art
Thousands of fascinating examples of Aboriginal rock paintings can be found in the Northern Territory, particularly in Kakadu National Park. Many of those paintings refer to the "Dream time": according to the Aborigines, it is the time when everything – rocks, trees, animals and humans – was created by supernatural beings. Two particular subjects are often represented on the paintings: the "Rainbow Serpent" – the ruler of the seasons – and the "Lightning Man" – the maker of lightning and thunder. The pictures in the caves are sacred. Only a limited number of visitors can enter the caves every year and no scientific tests are allowed.

But Aboriginal paintings of today can be found in shops or in art galleries and this art is getting more and more popular.

Remember and Practise

1 Le double comparatif

1. **Rappel : la formation des comparatifs.**

• **adjectif (ou adverbe) court, ou à deux syllabes et terminé en** *-y* (*happy*), *-er* (*clever*) → adj. + *-er*

Exemples : *faster, happier, nicer, cleverer*

• **adjectif (ou adverbe) de deux syllabes ou plus** → ***more*** + adj.

Exemples : ***more*** *pleasant*, ***more*** *interesting*

• ***many / much / a lot*** → ***more*** + nom

Exemples : ***more*** *shops*, ***more*** *time*

• ***few / not many*** → ***fewer*** + nom pluriel

Exemple : ***fewer*** *shops*

• **comparatifs irréguliers :**

good / well → ***better***
bad → ***worse***
far → ***farther / further***

2. **Le double comparatif** s'emploie pour traduire l'idée d'une **progression** (*« de plus en plus ... / de moins en moins ... »*) et se forme comme dans le tableau ci-dessous.

More and more changes are taking place in Australia.

▲ **Exprime ce qui change en utilisant un double comparatif, comme dans les exemples suivants:**

There is a lot of pollution in cities.
→ *Yes, there is more and more pollution.*

1. Children spend a lot of time watching TV.
2. Nowadays, people write few letters.
3. Not many young people like reading.
4. People try to spend less money on cigarettes.

It is difficult to find a parking place.
→ *Yes, it is getting more and more difficult to find a parking place.*

5. Traffic in big cities is bad.
6. Cars are comfortable nowadays.
7. Nowadays teenagers are tall.
8. Australian wine is good.

	« de plus en plus »	« de moins en moins »
nom dénombrable indénombrable	 ***more and more*** *cars* ***more and more*** *time*	 ***fewer and fewer*** *cars* ***less and less*** *time*
adjectif ou adverbe court long	 *faster and faster* ***more and more*** *interesting*	 ***less and less*** *interesting*

2 Le style indirect: le passage de *will* à *would*

He said that more and more restaurants would serve Australian wine.

• **Rappel:**

Lorsque l'on rapporte les paroles de quelqu'un en les introduisant par un verbe au passé (*he said / told / answered / asked ...*) le temps des verbes des paroles rapportées est modifié.

Exemple:

*He said, "I **am** in a hurry."*
→ *He **said** (that) he **was** in a hurry.*

• Ainsi ce qui est au futur est rapporté au futur dans le passé: l'auxiliaire modal ***will*** devient ***would***.

Exemple:

*He said, "I **will** be back at ten."*
→ *He **said** (that) he **would** be back at ten.*

▲ **Rapporte les paroles de ces deux dialogues en les introduisant par un verbe au passé.**

Paul: I want to go to Australia.
Lucy: When will you go there?
Paul: I'll leave as soon as I can.

Tom: Will you be at home after dinner?
Laura: I won't; I'm going out.
Tom: Don't forget to lock the door!
Laura: I won't forget.

3 Le *present perfect* avec *be + -ing*

What have they been doing?

1. Formation :

have / has been + -ing

Exemples :

*I **have been** runn**ing**.* (J'ai couru.)

*It **has been** rain**ing**.* (Il a plu.)

2. Emploi :

• Cette forme associe deux valeurs :

- celle de la forme en ***be + -ing*** qui traduit **une activité dans son déroulement.**

- celle du *present perfect (have* + participe passé) qui traduit un **constat présent**;

C'est pourquoi la forme *have been + -ing* est utilisée pour parler d'une **activité qui vient de se terminer et dont on constate les effets présents.**

• Cette forme est incompatible avec des verbes qui ne traduisent pas une activité en déroulement, tels que *know, like, hate,* etc.

▲ **Imagine l'activité qui vient de se passer et complète les énoncés à l'aide des verbes suivants :**

• fight • work • cook • try • use • smoke • peel

1. I ... fish, that's why there is such a strong smell in the house.
2. I ... all day, so I haven't had time to call you.
3. Look! The cat's eye is bleeding, she ... with another cat.
4. Mike ... to repair his motorbike all afternoon.
5. I am not crying for real, don't worry, it's just because I ... onions.
6. What an awful smell in the car! Someone ... a cigar.
7. Why is my computer on? Who ... it?

4 Le *present perfect* avec *be + -ing for ... / since ...*

He's been driving for 7 hours.

Lorsque l'**on associe à un *present perfect*** :

• **la durée** d'une activité (*for two days, for half an hour, for a long time, all day ...*)

• **le point de départ** de l'activité (*since yesterday, since I was ten, since WWII ...*)

• ou **la question en *How long*,**

cela indique que **l'activité dure encore.**

Compare les exemples suivants :

It has been raining.
Il a plu.

*It has been raining **since this morning**.*
Il pleut depuis ce matin.

I have been painting.
J'ai fait de la peinture.

*I have been painting **for an hour**.*
Je peins depuis une heure. / Cela fait une heure que je suis en train de peindre.

▲ **Construis des énoncés en mettant le verbe au *present perfect* avec *be + -ing*, puis traduis chacune des phrases en français.**

1. - My elder brother is unemployed.
   - How long ... he ... a job? [look for]
2. We ... here for ten years. [live]
3. I am freezing. I ... in the rain. [wait]
4. I ... to start my car for ten minutes. Can you help me push it? [try]
5. I'm tired because I ... late. [work]
6. - You know what? Alex is going out with Emma!
   - Is he? How long ... he ... with her? [go out]
7. My hands are dirty. I ... [garden]
8. Cassandra plays the piano very well. She ... the piano for six years. [play]
9. How long ... you ... this exercise? [do]

Réutilise tes connaissances

▲ **Dis en anglais.**

1. De plus en plus de fermiers australiens utilisent des hélicoptères.
2. Les pompiers sont épuisés parce qu'ils ont essayé d'éteindre un feu de brousse.
3. Les Aborigènes habitent en Australie depuis 50 000 ans.
4. Je lui ai demandé combien de temps il passerait à Sydney.

▲ **Imagine un début ou une suite aux phrases suivantes.**

1. ... more and more popular.
2. ... since I was born.
3. ... for a long time.
4. Our Australian guide told us that ...

7 Visit Ireland, the Emerald Isle

Objectifs

1— *Le past perfect*
What had they already done?
Le style indirect : le passage du *present perfect* au *past perfect*

2— L'hypothèse au passé
What might have happened if things had been different?

3— L'expression du regret
I wish I had taken waterproof clothing.

How much do you know about Ireland?

QUIZ

Look at the map and read the information.
Then do the quiz in your workbook. ▸ **WB, p. 112**

population: Northern Ireland: 1.6 million inhabitants
Republic of Ireland: 4 million inhabitants

SAINT PATRICK

456 AD
Saint Patrick converted the Irish to Christianity. The Irish built monasteries all over Ireland. But most of them were raided by the Vikings in the 8th century.

THE FIRST ENGLISH COLONY

16th century
Under the Tudors, Ireland became England's first colony. English protestant settlers were given rich lands in the North whereas Irish Catholics were dispossessed of their lands.

OLIVER CROMWELL

1649
Cromwell, England's Lord Protector, took an army to Ireland and crushed the Irish Catholics. They were banned from Parliament, forbidden to go to Catholic schools and considered as second-class citizens. Thousands of them were even sold as slaves to the West Indies.

THE GREAT FAMINE

1846-1849
For three consecutive years the potato crop – the sole source of food for the Irish peasants – failed. As a result, out of five million people, one million died of starvation and another million emigrated, mostly to the US.

THE EASTER RISING

1916
After "the Easter Rising"– an attempt by nationalists to proclaim Ireland a republic – fifteen Irish republican leaders were executed by the English. They became heroes and martyrs. More and more Irish, shocked by such violence, supported the idea of an independent Ireland.

THE REPUBLIC OF IRELAND

1921
Ireland was partitioned under two governments. Northern Ireland – Ulster – remained in the UK. Southern Ireland – Eire – became an independent nation, later named the "Republic of Ireland".

"THE TROUBLES"

Since 1972
In Northern Ireland riots have opposed Protestants – supported by the British army – and Catholics – supported by the IRA (Irish Republican Army).
Bombings, riots, and violent deaths have taken the lives of more than 3,400 people in this 30-year-long struggle.
Until now no peaceful solution has been found.

THE NEW DUBLINERS

the late 1990s
Ireland used to be a land of emigration with a high rate of unemployment. But since the turn of the 21st century, many computer companies have settled in Dublin, boosting its economy and creating many jobs. Nowadays Dublin has become a lively and dynamic city attracting young people and students from all over Europe.

1 What had they already done?

1. Look and comment. ▸ WB, p. 114

Last summer, Brian and Tessa went on a trip around Ireland with a few friends.

Look at the dates on their photographs and make comments as in these examples:

*When they visited Dublin, they **hadn't seen** the Giants' Causeway yet.*
*When they saw a hurling match, they **had** already **visited** Dublin.*

[see] a hurling match

[see] the Giants' Causeway

[walk along] the Cliffs of Moher

[visit] Dublin

[hike along] the Ring of Kerry

[take] a cruise down the river Shannon

[see] a "round tower"

2. Listen and comment.

Listen to two people talking and comment about what they are saying. ▶ WB, p. 115

3. What about you? ▶ WB, p. 115

Complete the sentences:

When I was ten, I had already ... / I had never ...

The verbs in the box may help you.

- take a plane / a taxi / a bus by myself
- travel abroad / by myself / abroad by myself
- go to the theatre / to a concert
- go to the seaside / to the mountains
- visit a museum ...

4. Reported speech. ▶ WB, p. 115

Report what Brian said during his trip, as in this example:

*He said it **was** the first time he **had visited** Ireland.*

*It **is** the first time I'**ve visited** Ireland.*

*It **is** the first time I'**ve seen** traditional Irish dances.*

*It **is** the first time I'**ve fished** for salmon.*

*It **is** the first time I'**ve listened** to Celtic music.*

*It **is** the first time I'**ve drunk** Irish coffee.*

Listening

Oral practice

La terminaison *-ity*

■ Ecoute et repère les syllabes accentuées dans les mots suivants :

- *identity*
- *majority*
- *nationality*
- *Christianity*
- *community*
- *opportunity*

Quelle règle peux-tu tirer ?

■ Fais l'exercice d'entraînement dans ton *workbook*. ▶ WB, p. 116

1. Listening comprehension.

Listen to the conversation and do the task in your workbook. ▶ WB, p. 117

2. Summary.

Now, sum up the story with the help in your workbook. ▶ WB, p. 117

2 What might have happened if things had been different?

1. Make comments. ▸ WB, pp. 118-119

Use the information and the verbs given to say:

• what Judy's life was like, until she lived in Beverly Hills (the boxes along the green line);

• what wouldn't have happened if things had been different, as in this example:

*If Judy's parents **hadn't had** cousins in America, they **wouldn't have** emigrat**ed** to America.*

• what might have happened if things had been different (the purple "clouds") as in this example:

*If Judy's parents **hadn't had** cousins in America, they **might have** emigrat**ed** to Australia.*

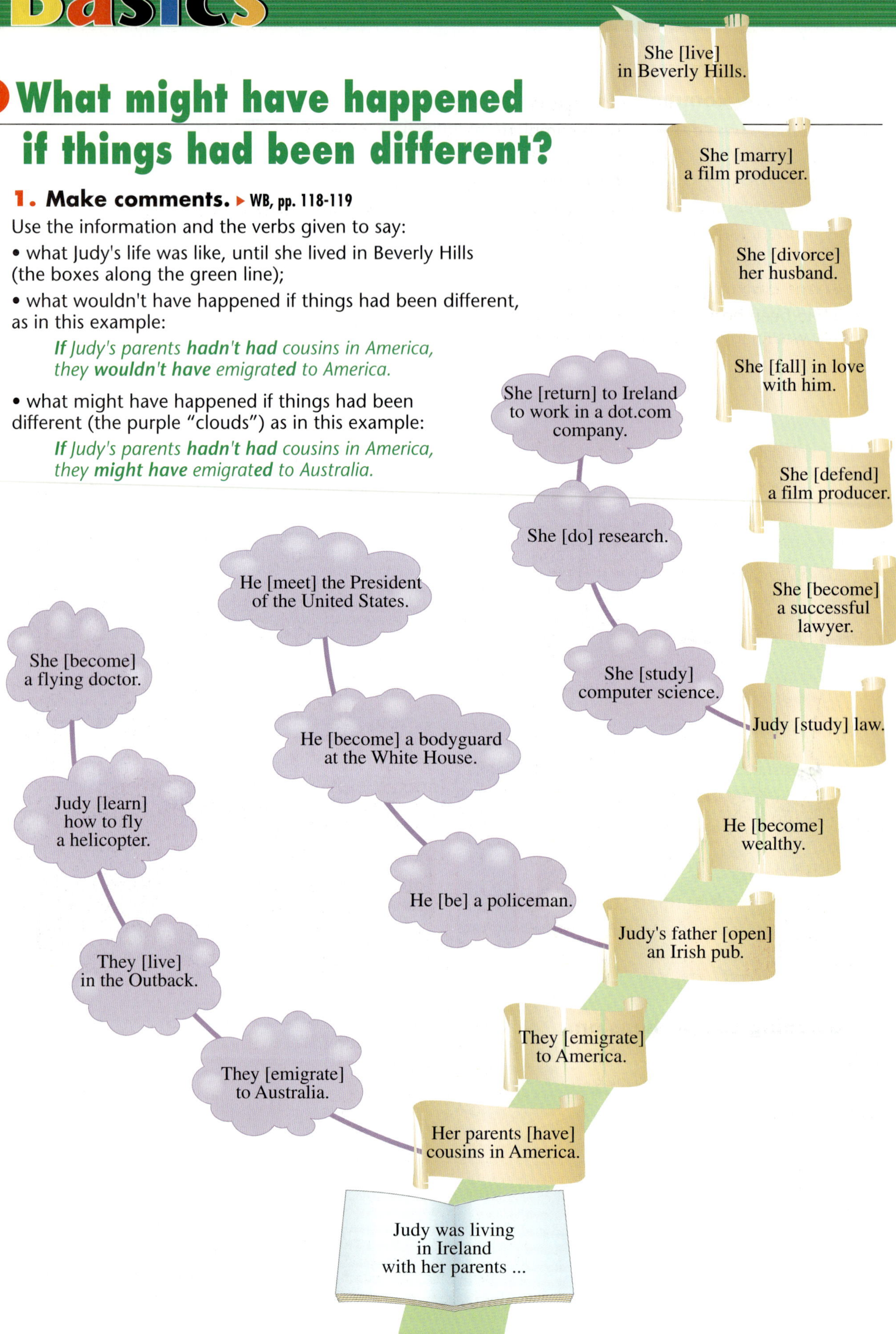

2. What wouldn't have happened? ▸ WB, p. 119

Look at the time line on page 97 to complete the following sentences:

- *If the Irish **hadn't been converted** to Christianity, ...*
- *If the potato crop **hadn't failed** for three consecutive years, ...*
- *If Irish republican leaders **hadn't been executed** by the English after the Easter Rising, ...*
- *If computer companies **hadn't settled** in Dublin, ...*

3. What about you? ▸ WB, p. 119

If you had been born in the 19th century or in another country, your life would have been different. Say how.

Listening

1. Listening comprehension.

Listen to the conversation and do the task in your workbook.

▸ WB, pp. 120-121

2. Summary.

Now, sum up the story with the help in your workbook.

▸ WB, p. 121

Oral practice

Les prononciations de *have*

■ Lorsque *have* est un verbe, il ne peut être en forme réduite, et se prononce toujours [hæv].
Ecoute et répète les expressions suivantes :
I have *a shower every morning.*
You can't have *that.*

■ Lorsque *have* est un auxiliaire suivi d'un participe passé, il se prononce généralement en forme réduite [əv], même si ce mot est écrit sous sa forme entière.
Ecoute et répète les expressions suivantes :
They have *done ...*
He would have *said ...*
You might have *become ...*
I wouldn't have *emigrated ...*

■ Fais l'exercice d'entraînement dans ton *workbook.* ▸ WB, p. 120

3 I wish I had taken waterproof clothing!

1. Make comments. ▸ WB, p. 122

With a classmate, make comments using the verbs under each drawing. Say what Steve and Clara wish (marked in the green boxes) or what they regret (marked in the purple boxes).

Begin each sentence with *I wish ...*, as in these examples:

***I wish I had** something warm to drink.*
***I wish I weren't** out in the rain.*
***I wish I had taken** waterproof clothing.*

1

[have] something warm to drink
[not be] out in the rain
[take] waterproof clothing

2

[have] a map
[take] the car

3

[come] by plane
[not be] seasick

4

feet [not hurt]
[take] comfortable shoes

5

[not forget] my aspirin
[not have] such a bad headache

6

[can] dry my hair
[buy] an adapter plug

7

[there be] fewer tourists
[book] a room

3. Listening comprehension. → Test

IMMIGRATION ▸ WB, p. 123

be homesick	*avoir le mal du pays*
miss	*s'ennuyer de*
I miss my family.	*Ma famille me manque.*
adapt (to)	*s'adapter (à)*
expect	*s'attendre à*
trust	*faire confiance à*
mother tongue	*langue maternelle*
foreigner ['fɒrənə]	*étranger (nom)*
foreign	*étranger (adjectif)*
harassment	*harcèlement, brimades*
rejection	*rejet*
prejudice ['predʒʊdɪs]	*préjugé(s)*
racism ['reɪsɪzm]	*racisme*
newcomer	*nouvel(le) arrivant(e)*
native country ['neɪtɪv 'kʌntrɪ]	*pays natal*
work permit	*permis de travail*
accommodation [əˌkɒmə 'deɪʃən]	*logement*
embassy	*embassade*
customs ['kʌstəmz]	*douane*
border	*frontière*

1. Listen and repeat.
Listen and repeat the words from the list.

2. Listen and answer.
Listen to the questions and give the right answer.

3. A hidden message.

'reɪsɪzm 'ʃʊdnt bi: 'tɒləreɪtɪd

Coin New Words

You can coin new words by combining an adjective and a noun *+ed*, as in these examples:

open-minded	**big-hearted**	**left-handed**
red-haired	**blue-eyed**	**old-fashioned**

Now, do the exercise in your workbook. ▸ WB, p. 124

AN IMMIGRANT IN FRANCE

Conall Carr is Irish. He grew up with his eight brothers and sisters in Donegal, on the western coast of Ireland. Now he runs an Irish pub in the centre of Paris.

▸ WB, p. 125

1. What is it like to be an Irish immigrant in France?

Actually, I feel quite at home. There used to be few Irish people in France, compared to London or New York. But now Irish pubs are becoming more and more popular in France, that's why there are quite a lot of Irishmen here. We don't have the problems of harassment and rejection that many immigrants have. But, as soon as I open my mouth people know I'm a foreigner!

2. Have you always had a strong interest in travel and in languages?

My mother tongue was Gaelic, and I was brought up bilingual. Perhaps having two languages from a young age is an advantage. It made me want to speak other languages by travelling.

3. What do you miss?

Well, sometimes you do get homesick, you do miss your own country and hearing and speaking your own language. When you live in a foreign country and start to speak another language, your mother tongue gets rusty **unless** you speak it at home with your family!

4. Your life would have been different if you had never left Ireland, wouldn't it?

Yes, it would have been totally different, certainly. I wouldn't have been able to speak foreign languages, and I might not have felt so European. But I presume I would have stayed in the same profession. I started off in the hotel business, so I suppose I would have continued because it's the best passport to travel. There's a great need for trained staff all over the world. Even if I hadn't emigrated I would have spent a lot of time working abroad.

5. Ireland has changed a lot these last few years, hasn't it?

Yes, it has! We used to be a country of emigrants, but now many young people from all over the world come to Ireland to work as technicians and engineers in computer companies. I wish more companies settled in the west of Ireland, because it's not easy to find a job there **unless** you work in the tourist business.

6. What would you say to young French people about living abroad?

I think all young people should go and live abroad– not just for a month or two but for a few years– to become more open-minded and to learn to accept other ideas and cultures. And why not in Ireland?

From: mdoherty@jobs.ire.com
To: Chloe McCourt@sununiv.com
Subject: Request for employment
Date: Thu, 6 Feb 2003 08:57:58+0000

Thank you for your interest in jobs in our area. There are currently no vacancies, but please check our web page regularly for job opportunities in the future.

unless ...

It's not easy to find a job there ... you work in the tourist business.

Class work

Linking word. ▸ WB, p. 126

Read the caption under the two pictures above. Then read the phrases in A and B about Ireland, and connect them with *unless.*

A

1. You won't enjoy a hurling match,
2. Don't plan to tour Ireland in a horse-drawn carriage,
3. You won't be allowed to fish for salmon,
4. You won't be able to see the Giants' Causeway,

B

1. ... you have a fishing licence.
2. ... you have plenty of time.
3. ... you go to Northern Ireland.
4. ... you have been explained the rules before.

Role play.

Imagine you are one of the people you have just read about. Follow your teacher's instructions.

What about you?

Answer the questions your teacher is going to ask about immigrating.

Discussion.

Do you agree or disagree?

Having two languages from a young age is an advantage.

All young people should go and live abroad.

Personal expression

Get ready for a talk.

You may know or you may have heard of people who have immigrated to France. Say where they came from, why they left their countries, and what difficulties they have encountered.

Your teacher may record you.

Writing task.

If you chose to emigrate, which country would you choose?

Explain your choice.
▸ WB, p. 127

Listening → Test

Saint Patrick's day

The Irish national holiday is celebrated by the Irish throughout the world on March 17th. That day people wear a green ribbon or a shamrock leaf. And since there are more Irish in America than in Ireland itself, that day, the Irish Prime Minister goes to Washington and offers the President of the United States an Irish-made crystal bowl full of shamrocks.

The shamrock is said to have been used by Saint Patrick to explain Christianity to the Irish: the three leaves represent the Holy Trinity (the Father, the Son and the Holy Ghost).

Irish traditional music

Traditional music and Irish dances are very much alive in Ireland. Wherever you go, especially in pubs, you can hear people singing.

Popular folk instruments are the tin whistle – a small flute made of tin –, the violin, and a large drum called "bodhram". The Celtic harp is a symbol of Eire. It used to be played by the bards who were admired both for their learning and their music.

Celtic sports

In 1884 the Gaelic Athletic Association was created to encourage traditional Irish sports instead of "foreign" sports such as cricket and soccer.

Two sports are very popular: hurling, which is a sort of hockey, and Gaelic football, which is a sort of rugby. Both finals, fast and exciting spectacles, take place every year in Dublin in September.

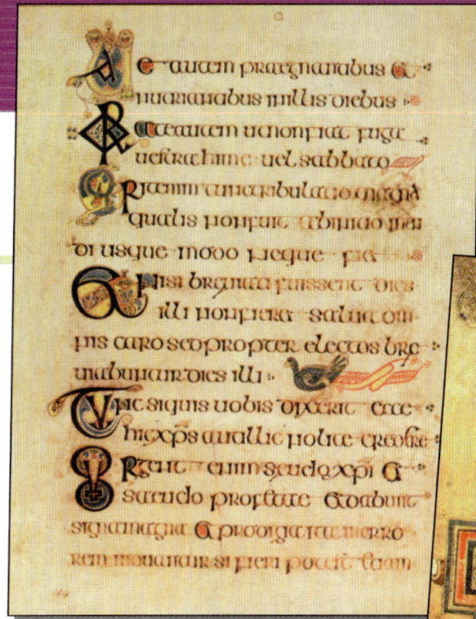

The Irish and Christianity

In the 7th and 8th centuries there were many monasteries throughout Ireland where monks illuminated manuscripts written in Latin.
The *Book of Kells* which can be seen in Dublin is one of the most beautifully illuminated manuscripts in the world.
At that time, the Irish also sculpted Celtic crosses with illustrated scenes from the Bible which can still be found everywhere in the countryside.
Catholicism is still very much alive in the Republic of Ireland: 90% of the population is Catholic.

From bards to Nobel Prize winners

The Irish have a way with words: they love to talk, tell stories and have fun with words. They inherited the Celtic tradition of oral literature transmitted by the bards – poets who composed and recited verses celebrating the legendary exploits of heroes.
Many world-famous writers, like Oscar Wilde, are Irish, and some of them – George Bernard Shaw, Samuel Beckett, William Butler Yeats among others – won the Nobel Prize for Literature.

Irish Gaelic

Irish Gaelic is a Celtic language belonging to the same family as Welsh, Breton and Scottish Gaelic. It was spoken by the whole of Ireland.

After the massive emigration due to the Great Famine, many associations were created to stop the decline of Irish Gaelic. The Republic of Ireland is bilingual: documents and road signs are in both Irish and English, and Irish Gaelic is compulsory in primary and secondary schools. Irish is also one of the official languages of the European Union.

Irish names are not always pronounced the way they are written. For example, the name *Sean* is pronounced [ʃɒːn], the town *Dun Laoghaire* is pronounced [dʌn ˈlɜːri].

Remember and Practise

1 Le *past perfect*

A partir d'un **point de repère temporel dans le passé** (une date, une heure, un moment, un événement, ...), il est possible de parler de:

- ce que l'**on a fait** à ce moment-là; le verbe est alors au **prétérit**.

Exemple:

This morning I had a shower at 7.00.
Ce matin j'ai pris une douche à 7 heures.

- ce que l'**on avait déjà fait** ou **pas encore fait** à ce moment-là ; le verbe est alors au *past perfect:* (auxiliaire *had* + participe passé)

Exemples:

*At 7.00 I **had** already **had** breakfast.*
À 7 heures, j'avais déjà pris mon petit-déjeuner.

*At 7.00 I **hadn't made** my bed yet.*
À 7 heures, je n'avais pas encore fait mon lit.

What had they already done?

▲ **Complète ces phrases en utilisant le verbe proposé soit au prétérit soit au *past perfect*.**

1. Last year we ... [go] on a school trip to London. I ... [never visit] London before. It was the first time I ... [travel] abroad.
2. During my trip around Ireland, I ... [take] a cruise down the river Shannon. It was great because it was the first time I ... [take] a cruise.
3. When I ... [arrive] at school this morning, I ... [not finish] my English homework yet, so I ... [finish] it during a free period.

2 Le style indirect : le passage du *present perfect* au *past perfect*

He said it was the first time he had visited Ireland.

Lorsque l'on rapporte les paroles de quelqu'un avec un **verbe introducteur au passé, ces paroles rapportées** sont elles-mêmes **au passé**.

- Quand le verbe est au présent au style direct, il est au prétérit au style indirect.

Exemple:

*He said, "I **have** a big backpack."*
*→ He said (that) he **had** a big backpack.*

- Quand le verbe est au *present perfect* au style direct, il est au *past perfect* au style indirect.

Exemple:

*He **said**, "I **have** never **been** to Ireland."*
*→ He **said** (that) he **had** never **been** to Ireland.*

▲ **Mets les deux dialogues suivants au style indirect en utilisant des verbes introducteurs au prétérit (*said, asked, answered*).**

Ann's mother: Ann, have you done your homework?
Ann: Not yet.
Ann's mother: When do you intend to do it?
Ann: I'll do it as soon as I've done my nails.

Kate: How long have you been doing classical ballet dancing?
Lucy: I've been dancing for ten years. I've always dreamt of becoming a professional dancer.

3 L'hypothèse au passé

What might have happened if things had been different?

1. Pour exprimer une **hypothèse dans le passé** (si les choses s'étaient passées ainsi), on utilise la structure :

If + sujet + verbe au *past perfect*

Exemple:

***If** her parents **hadn't had** cousins in America, ...*
Si ses parents n'avaient pas eu de cousins en Amérique, ...

2. Pour exprimer la **conséquence résultant** de cette hypothèse dans le passé (ce qui serait arrivé), on emploie le conditionnel passé :

would(n't) have + participe passé

Exemple:

*... they **wouldn't have** emigrated to America.*
... ils n'auraient pas émigré en Amérique.

3. Pour exprimer une **conséquence simplement possible** de cette hypothèse dans le passé (ce qui se serait **peut-être** passé), on emploie:

might have + participe passé

Exemple:

*... they **might have** emigrated to Australia.*
... ils auraient peut-être émigré en Australie.

1 Dis ce qui se serait passé si les choses avaient été différentes. Puis traduis ces phrases en français.

1. If the Vikings ... [not raid] the monasteries, the Irish ... [not build] round towers.
2. If the Romans ... [settle] in Ireland, Latin ... [have] more influence on the Irish language.
3. Last summer, if we ... [have] more time, we ... [spend] two days hiking along the Ring of Kerry.
4. If I ... [be] in Dublin on March 17th, I ... [be] able to see the parade in the streets.

2 Complète les phrases ci-dessous en imaginant ce qui se serait peut-être passé dans les situations suivantes :

1. If it hadn't rained so much, ...,
2. If I had bought a Lottery ticket, ...
3. If no one had helped me, ...
4. If she had not met him, ...

4 L'expression du regret

I wish I had taken waterproof clothing.

1. Le prétérit «modal» et le *past perfect* «modal »:

Comme l'imparfait et le plus-que-parfait du français, les formes du prétérit et du *past perfect* peuvent respectivement être utilisées pour traduire une hypothèse présente ou passée.

Exemple:

If I lost my bag, ... / If I had lost it, ...
Si je perdais mon sac, ... / Si je l'avais perdu, ...

2. Pour exprimer **un regret** concernant :

- ce qui se passe, on utilise la structure :

I wish + sujet + prétérit

Exemple:

*I wish it **didn't rain** so much!*
Si seulement il ne pleuvait pas autant!

- ce qui ne s'est pas passé, on utilise la structure:

I wish + sujet + *past perfect*

Exemple:

*I wish I **had taken** warm clothes!*
Si seulement j'avais pris des vêtements chauds!

3. Rappel:

Pour le verbe *be,* on emploie ***were*** à toutes les personnes.

Exemple:

*I wish I **were** there.*
Si seulement j'étais là!

1 Transforme chacune des phrases ci-dessous en utilisant *I wish* suivi d'un prétérit. (Attention au changement des formes affirmatives en formes négatives et réciproquement).

1. I can't speak English fluently.
2. My parents don't have time to help me with my homework.
3. I am not very tall.
4. I live in a big city (but I don't like it).

2 Transforme chacune des phrases ci-dessous en utilisant *I wish* suivi d'un *past perfect*.

1. I've spent all my pocket-money.
2. I didn't see the concert.
3. She didn't give me her phone number.
4. I've eaten too much chocolate. Now I feel sick.

Réutilise tes connaissances

1 Dis en anglais.

1. Quand je suis arrivé(e), ils avaient déjà fini de dîner.
2. Si j'avais su, je ne serais pas venu(e).
3. Si tu m'avais appelé(e), je t'aurais peut-être aidé(e).
4. Si seulement j'étais meilleur(e) en langues!
5. Si seulement j'avais été là!

2 Réécris ces questions en mettant les mots dans le bon ordre.

1. lost / you / have / what / done / you / would / if / had / passport / your / ?
2. you / your / called / have / would / embassy/ ?
3. police station / to / you / would / the nearest / have / gone / ?

Ron B. Kitaj, *Joe Singers enfant*, 1980

Story time

Sunday Bloody Sunday

Captain Cook's Voyages of Discovery Across the Globe

Frankenstein

Not dressed like that, you don't!

Sunday Bloody Sunday ▸ WB, pp. 131-133

On Sunday 30 January 1972, some 20,000 civilians marched through the town of Derry in Northern Ireland. They were protesting against the policy of the English government which imprisoned suspected IRA sympathisers without trial. While they were demonstrating, the English army fired on the unarmed marchers, killing fourteen people, some shot in the back. Those responsible for this massacre were never punished.

In 1981 another tragic event took place in Ulster: ten Republican prisoners who had demanded to be recognised as political prisoners and not as terrorists went on a hunger strike and died. Among them was Bobby Sands, an elected MP.

The popular Irish group *U2* composed the song "Sunday Bloody Sunday" in 1983. It sums up a decade of passion, hatred and violence.

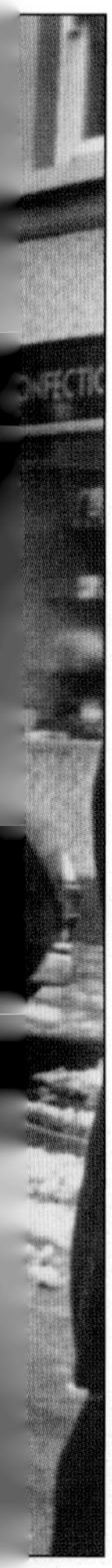

I can't believe the news today.
I can't close my eyes and go away.
How long, how long must we sing this song?
How long? How long?
'cause tonight we can't be as one. Tonight.

Broken bottles under children's feet.
Bodies strewn across the dead end streets.
But I won't heed the battle call.
It puts my back up,
Puts my back up against the wall.

Sunday, bloody Sunday.
Sunday, bloody Sunday.

How long, how long must we sing this song?
How long? How long?
'cause tonight we can't be as one.
Tonight.
Tonight.

Sunday, bloody Sunday.
Sunday, bloody Sunday.

And the battle's just begun.
There's many lost, but tell me, who has won?
The trenches dug within our hearts,
And mother's children, brothers, sisters torn apart.

Sunday, bloody Sunday.
Sunday, bloody Sunday.

How long, how long must we sing this song?
How long? How long?
'cause tonight we can't be as one.
Tonight.
Tonight.

Sunday, bloody Sunday.
Sunday, bloody Sunday.

Wipe the tears from your eyes.
Wipe your tears away.
Wipe your bloodshot eyes.

Sunday, bloody Sunday.
Sunday, bloody Sunday.

And it's true we are immune,
When fact is fiction and TV reality.
And today the millions cry.
We eat and drink while tomorrow they die.
The real battle's just begun.
To claim the victory Jesus won,
On Sunday, bloody Sunday.
Sunday, bloody Sunday.

SUNDAY BLOODY SUNDAY,
WORDS AND MUSIC BY U2.

Captain Cook's Voyages of Discovery Across the Globe ▸ WB, pp. 134-136

Cook's Early Life

James Cook was born in England, in 1728. As the son of a poor farm labourer, he grew up on a farm, worked in the fields and received very little formal education. At the age of 17, his love and fascination for the sea made him leave home. He became apprenticed to a family of ship owners. He educated himself, learned a lot about navigation and mathematics and soon went on his voyage on a coal ship, doing various jobs as an ordinary sailor.

At the age of 25 he was already an officer, and only three years later he was promoted Captain in the Merchant Marine. But he refused the title. Knowing that war with France was imminent, he chose to join the Royal Navy – as an ordinary sailor, once again. The Seven Years War with France broke out in 1756. And if Quebec fell to the English in 1763, it was thanks to the extremely detailed maps of the Canadian coastline and rivers drawn by Cook, who became an officer in the Royal Navy.

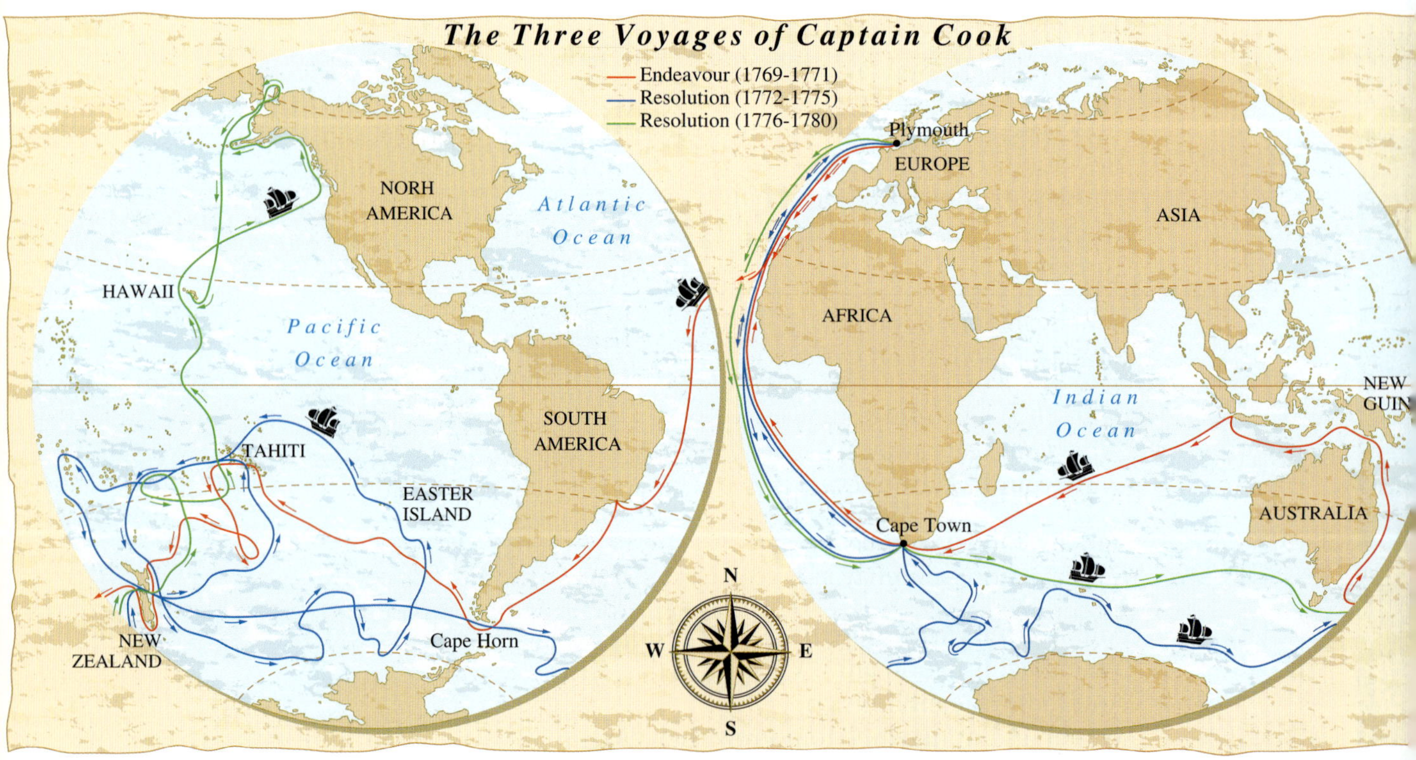

The 1st Voyage

In July 1769 the British Admiralty sent Cook to Tahiti aboard the *Endeavor*. It was the first British scientific expedition. On board were a hundred sailors and eleven scientists whose aim was to study wildlife. There was also live cattle, sheep, chickens and pigs; enough food and drink – including water and rum – for a whole year.

Officially, their aim was to observe the planet Venus during its transit across the sun. Actually, they also had a secret mission: to find the "great southern continent" that, according to some scientists, existed somewhere in the southern hemisphere. And the English hoped to find it before the French so that they could find new lands for future colonies.

The journey was long and tedious, the seas were often stormy and terribly dangerous. The crew did not encounter scurvy, the terrible disease that had taken so many sailors' lives in the past. Indeed Captain Cook, who knew that this disease was caused by lack of fruits and vegetables, made everyone eat sauerkraut at every meal – even though they all refused to even taste this strange-looking thing at first. However, the worst enemy they had to face was the cold. As they sailed across Cape Horn, two of the sailors froze to death.

They reached Tahiti. The scientific mission, however, was not successful: because they did not have glasses to protect their eyes from the rays of the sun, the scientists were unable to observe Venus.

Cook continued his voyage southward. He circumnavigated New Zealand and drew a map of the coastline which was so accurate and complete that it was used until the beginning of the 20th century! He sailed again and reached Australia where he identified the Great Barrier Reef. The scientists on board discovered a large number of plants and animals that were unknown to them such as the gum tree and the kangaroo.

Cook claimed all of eastern Australia for Britain. Then he continued westward and confirmed the existence of a new sea route between Australia and New Guinea before returning to England on July 13th, 1771.

The 2nd Expedition

One question remained: did another continent actually exist in the southern hemisphere?

Cook was promoted Commander and was asked to lead a second expedition, with two ships – the *Resolution* and the *Discovery*. This time he had with him a new instrument called the chronometer. Cook was the very first navigator in history to use this instrument to calculate the east-west position (or longitude) of a ship at sea in relation to Greenwich Mean Time. Ships today navigate in the same way.

Cook left England in 1772 to sail to Cape Town; then he continued south, crossing the Antarctic Circle. He was the first to sail so far south, and his crew had to fight against the terrible weather conditions – extreme cold, fog and fierce storms. They were exhausted. Then a huge ice pack prevented his ship from going any further. Cook had to turn back and head north once again. At this point, he could not accomplish the mission he was given – discovering a new continent.

But Cook did not get discouraged. He went on, sailing across the Pacific to return to Tahiti where he, as always, received a warm welcome from the people. On his way, he had discovered Easter Island and a host of other islands in the Pacific. But still no sign of the great southern continent! He sailed on to New Zealand. But there he learnt of the tragic death of the entire crew of the *Discovery*. They had been massacred and devoured by the Maoris. Overwhelmed by sadness and disappointment – for the Maoris had always welcomed him as a friend before – Cook left and returned to England in July, 1775.

The 3rd and Final Voyage

In the summer of 1776 Cook was selected to command a third expedition, this time to search for a northwest passage between the Pacific Ocean and the Atlantic Ocean. He and his crew, aboard the well named *Resolution* sailed South, past Cape Town, Tasmania and New Zealand, and then went on North across the South Pacific and the North Pacific Ocean. When they reached Bering Strait, between North America and Asia, they were supposed to sail east to reach Baffin Bay between Greenland and Canada. Again, a wall of ice blocked the way east, and Cook had to turn around and go back.

Cook then sailed to Hawaii, where he was welcomed like a god, and given innumerable gifts. That's why what happened next is so hard to understand: in 1779 Cook was killed, stabbed to death by the Maoris. They later expressed regret for this act, and many years after his death, they considered him as a god. Cook's crew buried the remains of their captain. They left the island a few days later and arrived in England in July, 1779.

Frankenstein

▸ WB, pp. 137-139

Mary Shelley (1797-1851) was the only daughter of a famous philosopher and novelist. Her mother died a few days after her birth and she was brought up by her father and her stepmother.

At the age of sixteen she ran away to France and Switzerland with Percy Shelley, a young poet of twenty-two – one of the most famous English Romantic poets – and her stepsister who was fifteen years old.

In 1816 she married Shelley and in the same year she began her most famous work, Frankenstein. *She was in Switzerland at Lake Geneva with her husband and another famous poet, Byron, and they had decided to compete in writing ghost-stories full of mystery and terror.*

When her book was published in 1818, she was only twenty-one years old.

I

My name is Victor Frankenstein. I was born in Geneva. At the age of eighteen I went to university where I studied chemistry and medicine. One day I realised that I could use the energy from lightning to discover the secrets of life, to give life to things ... or to people that were dead, and to create new living creatures.

So, I built a very tall mast on top of the roof of my laboratory. It would catch lightning and send electricity down to a machine in the laboratory. Then, I decided to make a body: I bought or stole pieces of human bodies, and slowly and carefully I put them all together.

I had wanted to make a beautiful man, but the face of the creature I had made was ugly. His skin was wrinkled and yellow, and his eyes were as yellow as his skin. His thin lips opened in a cruel smile. His legs and arms were huge: my creature was not a man, but a monster that looked terrible and frightening.

II

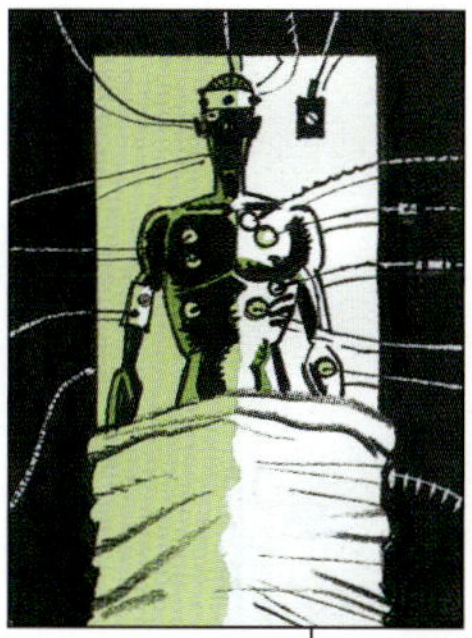

I connected the body to the wires from my machine.

Two days later I saw dark clouds in the sky, and I knew that a storm was coming. My mast began to do its work immediately, and the electricity from the lightning travelled down the mast to my machine.

At first, nothing happened. But after a few minutes I saw the creature's body begin to move. Slowly, terribly, the body came alive. The arms and legs began to move, and slowly the monster sat up. The dead body had been an ugly thing, but alive, it was much more horrible! I wanted to escape from it. I rushed out of the laboratory and ran into town. But the monster had escaped ...

A few months later, a young boy's body was found in the forest. It was my own brother who had been strangled.

III

Then I decided to go into the forest. A storm broke out, the lightning lit up the sky and I saw a huge figure standing in the rain. I knew at once what it was. It was the creature I had made. What was he doing there? The answer was too obvious: he was my brother's murderer. I realised then that I had created a monster. I felt fear for my family and I hated him. I saw him coming towards me. On his face was a look of deep sadness, but also of evil.

I hated him so much that at first I couldn't speak. But at last I said, "You are an evil creature. I will kill you if I can, because you have killed my brother."

The monster's yellow eyes looked at me. "I am the unhappiest creature in the world," he said. "You made me and you should love me and be kind to me, like a father. Your brother died because you did not love me. Why did you create me if you were not ready to love me? I am alone and miserable. People shout and throw stones at me. You must make another creature like me, a woman monster, and then I won't hurt anyone. Be kind to me, and I will learn to be kind and love others."

He was so miserable that I felt sorry for him. I said, "I shall do what you ask, but you must promise to live somewhere in the world where there are no people. You must promise you'll stay away from people." "I promise! I promise!", he cried. "Please, start your work. I shall watch you, and when you are ready, you can be sure I will come back." He turned away and left.

IV

Two months later, when most of my work was done, I realised I was making another monster perhaps even more evil than the first one.

One day, while I was working in my laboratory, I looked up and once again I saw the yellow eyes full of hate and evil. I went to the laboratory table where the new creature was lying. I pulled off the wires that attached her to my machine. Then I took a sharp knife and cut through the body that I had put together so carefully.

The monster saw me destroy his woman monster and cried," You have destroyed my hopes and happiness. You have left me with one feeling – hatred ... and only one wish – to destroy your happiness. Remember this: I shall be with you on your wedding night."

I sat and cried as I thought of my dear Elizabeth. I loved her so much! "I won't let the monster visit us on our wedding night, I shall fight and kill him before he can kill us," I thought.

V

Ten days later, Elizabeth and I were married. On our wedding night the wind howled and soon a great storm broke out over us. Every noise and every shadow frightened me. I asked Elizabeth to go to bed and decided to search for the monster. I searched every corner of the house – every dark doorway and staircase. I could not find him, and I began to hope that he had not followed us. But suddenly, I heard a loud and terrible scream coming from our room. Then – too late – I understood. I ran to our room. On the bed, Elizabeth lay still, in the cold sleep of death. I took her in my arms ... and saw the terrible marks of the murderer's fingers on her neck.

As I held Elizabeth close, I saw the monster watching me through the open window of the room. There was an evil grin on his face. I pulled my gun from my coat and fired at him. But I missed and he ran away.

VI

The awful news of Elizabeth's death killed my poor father, who died in my arms. From that moment on, my only goal was to find the monster and kill him.

One day, I heard his voice. "I want you to feel, day after day, the pain and misery you have given me." I ran towards the voice, but I saw the monster running away, too fast for me to catch. I followed him. He kept leaving me messages to tell me where he was.

In his last message, the monster told me that he was going north where the cold would hurt me and make me more miserable.

VII

I followed him to the cold icy lands of the North. At last, I saw his terrible figure standing in front of me. He turned to me and said, "I have felt much pain and unhappiness. I had asked you to create a friend for me. But you destroyed her. I had no family to love, so I destroyed yours. I knew I was doing evil but I couldn't stop myself. Now my own death is near. I shall go north, across the ice. I shall build a great fire and lie down on it and I shall be at peace."

Then he went away into the icy sea which carried him away, blanketing him in darkness.

Frankenstein, retold by Patrick Nobes,
Collection Oxford Bookworms, Oxford University Press

Not dressed like that, you don't! The diaries of a teenager... and her mother.

▶ WB, pp. 140-142

15th October

I hate my life. I have the dullest parents of anyone I know. Today was a typical example of life with my parents.

Just because I decided to go round to Sadie's tonight instead of working on my English assignment, I got the full works – "irresponsible", "devil-may-care attitude", etc. etc. What was I going to do when I reached the real world? Did I think GCSEs were going to fall out of trees into my lap? etc. etc. You would think it was a crime to go out and see your friends a couple of times a week. There are other things in life besides GCSEs. I tried to point this out, but they weren't prepared to listen to reason.

16th October

There's a new boy at school. His name's David Slater, and he's been living in Australia for the past ten years, apparently. He is GORGEOUS. He's very sporty, with lots of muscle and a great tan, too. He makes the other boys in the fourth year look like real wimps. And he has been put in my form! This has to give me a head start on the rest of the girls – who are already drooling at the mouth!

15th October

Rotten day. I've got a stinking cold, and feel almost as old as Jenny thinks I am. I looked forward to a quiet evening at home. No such luck. No sooner was I through the door than Jenny announced that she wouldn't be in for dinner. Mike pointed out that this was the fourth night running she's been out. He wondered when she was planning to catch up with her homework. Suddenly they were off, hammer and tongs, and I was in the middle of it all. I can never work out how that happens.

In the end she stomped off anyway and we were both too tired to stop her. Now Mike is looking all pinched and tense. It'll be ages before he gets to sleep.

7th November

Today I went down to the Saturday market with Sadie. I bought this great skirt – black and floaty, almost to the ground. I think it's silk or something, and it's at least forty years old, the lady who was selling it said. Sadie found some black lacy gloves on another stall – the sort that don't have fingers in them. Then we went back home and experimented with the make-up and stuff. Mum was down at the hospital and Dad took Jon to the football match, so we had the whole house to ourselves! We raided Mum's make-up in case she had anything useful – it was good for a laugh, but nothing else!

13th December

The school disco last night was FANTASTIC. Nearly didn't make it. Mum spotted my bag. I had to show them the black stuff – thank God Sadie was looking after the belts and chains or they wouldn't have let me leave. Cathy lent me her make-up and Sadie got our hair just right.

David Slater was really knocked out by the gear – asked me how long the make-up had taken, and whether we went for that look all the time. Then he asked me for a DANCE!!!! He's going to give me a call after Christmas. IS THIS A DATE?!

I was late from the disco – it took ages to get that stuff out of my hair. Mum talked about "responsibility" as usual, but who cares? David Slater has noticed me!

13th December

Jenny gave us a good laugh last night. It was the school disco. When it was time for her to leave, she came downstairs, wearing a very ordinary skirt and T-shirt. Behind her back was a bulging bag. I asked her what was in it and she went bright red. "Just me boots in case it rains." I kept a straight face and asked to see. Inside were some awful black rags, some tatty black lace, and the Doc Marten's we bought her for last year's walking holiday.

She was obviously going to change somewhere else and transform herself into one of those hideous Gothic creatures. Presumably Sadie or Catherine had the make-up and hair glue waiting. To find out it was just a costume was quite a relief. I had thought she might be planning to take drink or drugs. She was back late, so I gave her the usual lecture, but it was hard not to laugh.

Story time

4th January

Off on the annual culture trip to London. Only Mum could travel to London in the middle of the sales to go to art galleries. I tried to edge her towards Oxford Circus – I had my Christmas money still to spend – but no, we steamed off to the National Gallery. Feeling very noble, I didn't push the point. The poor old woman is trying her best. I didn't feel so noble after the fifty-ninth room of stuffy paintings, though. It took me about two minutes to look at the pictures – most of them looked much the same. I was so bored!

After lunch we went to the Tate Gallery. It proved to be Very Interesting Indeed. Not the pictures and stuff – what a load of rubbish! No, but there I was, trying to look interested, when I saw this fantastic boy. He was tall, and blond, but tanned. He was doing some kind of drawing in front of this great big painting that was all sorts of blobs and dots – I think it was a garden pond or something. Anyway, he looked up and smiled at me. My knees went all wobbly. I pretended to be really interested in the paintings. I went round the room slowly, staying by each painting for a long time, but he didn't look up again.

Ah well.

4th January

Today I took Jenny to London. I must admit I was tempted to skip the National and walk down to Oxford Street. Jenny said she wouldn't mind if I would rather go shopping instead. That was very noble of her and I was quite touched. But I wanted her to see the originals of the paintings she has only ever seen on posters or cards until now. Actually I was a bit disappointed by her reaction. I think she spent longer in the gift shop than she did in the entire gallery. But in the end, the trip proved fruitful. Jenny discovered the Impressionists. She became quite absorbed in Monet's "The Water Lilies" and in the other paintings around it, all impressionist. Culture is at last beginning to make its mark. I must remember to buy her a book about Monet for her birthday.

1st August

David dumped me today. I can hardly believe it. He's started to go out with Sadie. She's supposed to be my best friend. I go cold when I think of all the times I confided in her – all the things I told her about me and Dave. She says they couldn't help it – they just "fell in love". Dave didn't even have the guts to tell me himself. He wrote a note, and dropped it through the door. No mention of Sadie: just saying he was sorry. He'll always "like me as a friend". So I go charging off to Sadie, to cry on her shoulder. It was so humiliating. She thought I already knew, I must have suspected. Well I didn't. How could I? Now I face the rest of the school holiday alone. We had planned all sorts of things together – Dave and me, Sadie and me. Now I've got nothing. I'll never trust anyone again. I'm not going to suffer like this again for anybody.

When I got home from Sadie's, Mum was waiting. I cried and cried and she hugged me and didn't even ask what had happened. It was as if she knew. She was really great. She didn't tell me there were plenty more fish in the sea, like I expected. She made me a pot of tea and listened to everything I said without interrupting. Then she told me about the first boy who ever dumped her. It was centuries ago but she loved him at the time. When she was telling me how she'd felt, what they'd said to each other, it was just the sort of things I said and felt. It's amazing. Mum might be old, but she knows more than I thought she did.

Not dressed like that, you don't!
The diaries of a teenager... and her mother...

Outils méthodologiques

Savoir décrire une image

Savoir écrire une lettre

Savoir utiliser un dictionnaire

Savoir décrire une image

Les quatre étapes ci-dessous permettent de faire une description d'image :

*<u>On fait d'abord **une analyse objective** pour décrire:</u>*
1. ce qu'est le document,
2. ce qu'il montre et comment;

*<u>puis on fait **une analyse subjective** pour exprimer:</u>*
3. ce que ce document suggère,
4. ce qu'on en pense.

1. This document is ...

• a cartoon • a comic strip • a painting
• a photograph • a drawing • a poster
• an advertisement for ... • the cover of a book ...

• painted by ... • designed by / for ...
• drawn by ... • created by ... • taken by ...

• It is recent / It dates from ...

• There is a caption / a logo / a slogan / a brand name / underneath / next to ...

2. It shows ...

• Who? Where? When? What?
• What is happening?
• What colours are used?
• How are the different elements placed within the picture?
  - in the background / in the foreground
  - in the bottom left / top right corner
  - in the upper / lower part
• The people look ... / The place looks ...

3. This picture expresses ...

• happiness / loneliness / fear / sadness / anger / excitement / pleasure / the dangers of ... / the beauty of ...

• The message behind the picture is ...

• The target audience of the advert is teenagers / young adults / parents / housewives / executives / retired people ...

4. I like / I don't like this picture because ...

• I find this picture powerful / pleasant to look at / funny / odd / intriguing / ...

• It makes me feel ... / feel like ...

• It reminds me of ...

Edward Hopper, *Nighthawks,* 1942

Norman Rockwell, *Soda Fountain,* 1953

Savoir écrire une lettre

3407 North Linn St.
Chicago, IL 60246 **1**

10/03/04 **2**

Greatmeadow Youth Hostel **3**
New Arthur Place
Edinburgh

Dear Sirs, **4**

On September 28th, I spent the night in your youth hostel. When I got back home and unpacked I realized that I had forgotten a small bag containing several rolls of undeveloped film in my room. Would you be kind enough to **5** let me know if anything was found in room 29?

I appreciate your help and apologize for the inconvenience. I hope to hear from you soon and thank you once again.

Yours truly, **6**
John Mc Court
John Mc Court **7**

123, rue Boulanger
Paris 12^{e}, France **1**

March 14th, 2004 **2**

Ms. McCarthy **3**
Roma Pizza
Hadlow Road
London

Dear Ms. McCarthy, **4**

I am writing to you about the possibility of working as a waitress in your restaurant during the summer of 2004. I am 18 years old and will be available for work as soon as classes end in June. I would be able to work all through the summer, until the second weekend of September.

I have already had some experience working in restaurants. Last summer I had a part-time job in *Harry's*, on St. George's Street (London) where I served sandwiches and salads.

I am enclosing my resume. Please feel free to contact me if you should need any further information.

Thank you for considering my request. I am looking forward to **5** hearing from you at your earliest convenience.

Yours truly, **6**
Julie Dupont
Julie Dupont **7**

April 22nd, 2004 **2**

Dear Janet and Bob, **4**

Just a few lines to tell you how much I enjoyed my stay with you and how much I appreciated all the trouble you went to to make my trip so much fun! I had a wonderful time! And I'll never forget the delicious breakfasts!!

Mum and Dad send their regards. We're all looking forward to **5** *hearing from you soon.*

Love, **6**
Mathieu

L'adresse de l'expéditeur 1

A la différence des Français, les Anglais écrivent **l'adresse de l'expéditeur** en haut à droite sans mentionner le nom de celui-ci.

La date 2

Une date en chiffres se lit différemment selon que l'auteur de la lettre est américain ou britannique:
10/03/04 = the tenth of March (GB);
the third of October (US)

L'adresse du destinataire 3

L'adresse du destinataire se place à gauche.

Les formules de début 4

• **Une lettre personnelle** s'adressant à une connaissance, un membre de la famille, un ami:
- *Dear Mr Brown, Dear Betty, Dear Granny, Dear Uncle Bob,*

• **Une lettre officielle** s'adressant à un correspondant que l'on ne connaît pas ou à quelqu'un d'important: demande d'emploi, de renseignement, réservations, réclamations, remerciements, etc.:
- *Sir, / Madam,* (personne importante)
- *Dear Sir, / Dear Madam,* (sans nom de famille)
- *Dear Sirs,* (à une entreprise)

Quelques formules utiles 5

• pour demander quelque chose :
- *Would you be kind enough to ...*

• pour indiquer qu'on souhaite une réponse :
- *I look forward to hearing from you,*
- *Write back soon,* (fam.)

• pour transmettre ses salutations ou son amitié à quelqu'un d'autre que son correspondant:
- *Remember me to ...*
- *Say hello to ...*
- *Give my love to ...*

• pour remercier :
- *Just a line to say thank you for ...*
- *It was really nice of you to ...*
- *I can't thank you enough for ...*

Les formules de politesse 6

• Pour conclure **une lettre personnelle**:
- *All the best, / Best regards, / Best wishes,*
- *Regards to your family,*
- *Love, / Love to all,*
- XXX *(= lots of kisses)*

• Pour conclure une **lettre officielle**:
Yours truly, / Yours sincerely,

NB: ne pas oublier la virgule après les formules de début et de fin.

La signature 7

La signature (manuscrite) est suivie du prénom et du nom de celui qui écrit la lettre.

1 Lis des extraits de lettres (A) et retrouve à qui Simon les a adressées. (B).

A. Les extraits

1. Dear Sir,
Would you be kind enough to let me know if a blue jacket was found in room 305 ...

2. Dear Sirs,
In reply to your advertisement in the July issue of ... magazine ...

3. Get well soon! We all hope you'll be back home next week.

4. Say hello to Aunt Bess.

5. Sarah, ...

6. Dear Mr Anderson,
Would you be kind enough to send me the book I left ...

7. I'm looking forward to seeing you.

8. Remember me to your parents.

B. Les correspondants

a. his grandmother, who is in hospital
b. a hotel manager
c. his sister
d. a friend of his
e. his cousin
f. the owner of a holiday cottage
g. a magazine
h. his penfriend, who is coming this summer

2 Quelles formules utiliserais-tu pour:

1. remercier ta tante de son cadeau ?
2. demander à ton ami/e de te répondre rapidement ?
3. conclure ta lettre de demande de stage ?
4. transmettre ton amitié aux parents de ton correspondant ?

Savoir utiliser un dictionnaire

Quelques conseils utiles :

Il faut éviter :

– d'utiliser un dictionnaire de plus d'une dizaine d'années – les dictionnaires récents traduisent la langue courante de manière plus satisfaisante;

– d'utiliser un dictionnaire trop petit, à plus forte raison un dictionnaire électronique de poche qui ne donne pas suffisamment de précisions concernant l'usage des mots.

Il faut lire la rubrique entière pour vérifier les différents sens et ne pas s'arrêter à la première traduction.

grain /gʀɛ̃/ NM **a** *[de blé, riz, maïs, sel]* grain ◆ **le(s) ~(s)** *(= céréales)* (the) grain ◆ **~ d'orge** grain of barley, barleycorn ◆ **donner du ~ aux poules** to give grain to the chickens ◆ **alcool** *ou* **eau-de-vie de ~(s)** grain alcohol ◆ **le bon ~** *(Rel)* the good seed ◆ **cela leur a donné du ~ à moudre** *(matière à réflexion)* it gave them food for thought, it gave them something to chew over; *(travail)* it kept them occupied *ou* busy for a while ◆ **mettre son ~ de sel** * to put *ou* stick one's oar in * *(Brit)*, to put in one's two cents * *(US)*; → **poulet, séparer**

b *[de café]* bean ◆ **café en ~s** coffee beans, unground coffee ◆ **~ de raisin** grape ◆ **~ de cassis** blackcurrant ◆ **~ de poivre** peppercorn ◆ **poivre en ~s** whole pepper, peppercorns ◆ **moutarde en ~s** whole grain mustard

c *[de collier, chapelet]* bead; *(Méd = petite pilule)* pellet

d *(= particule) [de sable, farine, pollen]* grain; *[de poussière]* speck ◆ **~ de sable** *(fig)* blip *, glitch * ◆ **il suffit d'un ~ de sable pour tout bloquer** one blip * *ou* glitch * is enough to bring everything grinding to a halt

e ◆ **un ~ de** *(= un peu de) [+ fantaisie]* a touch of; *[+ bon sens]* a grain *ou* an ounce of ◆ **il n'y a pas un ~ de vérité dans ce qu'il dit** there's not a grain *ou* scrap of truth in what he says ◆ **il a un (petit) ~** * he's a bit touched *, he's not quite all there * ◆ **il faut parfois un petit ~ de folie** it sometimes helps to have a touch of madness *ou* to be a bit eccentric

f *(= texture) [de peau]* texture; *(Photo)* grain ◆ **à ~ fin** *[bois, roche]* fine-grained ◆ **à gros ~s** coarse-grained ◆ **travailler dans le sens du ~** to work with the grain

g *(= averse brusque)* heavy shower; *(Naut = bourrasque)* squall ◆ **essuyer un ~** to run into a squall; → **veiller**

h *(†† = poids)* grain; *(Can)* grain *(0.0647 gramme)*

COMP ▷ **grain de beauté** mole, beauty spot ▷ **grain de plomb** leadshot *(NonC)*

Le dictionnaire français - anglais

1. Les homophones

Certains mots se prononcent de la même façon mais n'ont ni la même orthographe ni le même sens. Assure-toi de la bonne orthographe du mot que tu recherches.

Exemples :

- ou, où, houx, houe
- cour, cours, court, courre

Complète la traduction des phrases suivantes :

1. **Où** veux-tu que je mette le **houx**? Sur la table **ou** sur la cheminée?
   ... do you want me to put the ... : on the table ... on the mantlepiece?
2. Les élèves restent dans la **cour** un **court** instant entre deux **cours**.
   The pupils stay in the ... for a ... time between two ...

2. Les abréviations

La page des abréviations se trouve en général au début de ton dictionnaire. Elles peuvent être différentes selon le dictionnaire. Voici les plus courantes qui te renseignent sur :

1. la catégorie grammaticale :

nature du mot :	ce que le dictionnaire indique :
• nom masculin	**nm**
nom féminin	**nf**
• adjectif	**adj**
• adverbe	**adv**
• préposition	**prep**
• verbe transitif *(= suivi d'un complément d'objet direct)*	**vt**
• verbe intransitif *(= suivi d'un complément d'objet indirect)*	**vi**
• indénombrable	**NonC**

2. le registre de langue:

• langage familier	***Fam.*** ou ***F.***
• langage littéraire	**liter**
• langage péjoratif	**péj**

3. le domaine d'utilisation:

• juridique	(Jur)
• botanique	(Bot)
• médical	(Méd)
• scolaire	(Scol)
• militaire	(Mil)
• scientifique	(Sci)
• informatique	(Comput)
• politique	(Pol)
• commercial	(Comm)

1 Donne la catégorie grammaticale des homonymes suivants, puis traduis les phrases :

1. Nous avons mangé du poisson **cru**.
2. Je ne l'ai pas **cru**.
3. Elle porte des **collants** noirs.
4. Mes doigts sont **collants**.
5. Les filles sont plus **mûres** que les garçons.
6. Nous avons cueilli des **mûres**.

2 Utilise un dictionnaire pour compléter les phrases avec les bonnes traductions.

4. Des kiwis, des raisins, des avocats.
   Kiwis, grapes, ...
5. Il est avocat.
   He is a ...
6. J'ai mangé une pêche.
   I ate a ...
7. La pêche est interdite.
   ... is forbidden.
8. Je fais les courses.
   I do the ...
9. Il a gagné plusieurs courses.
   He's won several ...

3 Indique le registre de langue des titres de films suivants :

1. Prends l'oseille et tire-toi!
2. Les Vestiges du jour
3. Le Père Noël est une ordure.
4. Le Glaive et la Balance
5. Vos gueules les mouettes!

4. Le mot-à-mot

Il ne faut pas chercher à traduire mot-à-mot à tout prix. Certaines expressions (les proverbes en particulier) ont un équivalent assez éloigné d'une langue à l'autre.

Exemple :

Ce n'est pas la mer à boire!

~~*It's not the sea to drink*~~*!*

= *It's not asking the impossible.*

Trouve dans un dictionnaire la bonne traduction pour :

1. Elle a une dent contre moi.
2. Il a pris ses jambes à son cou.
3. Ça m'a coûté les yeux de la tête.
4. J'ai une faim de loup.
5. J'ai mal au cœur.

5. Le pronom *one*

Le dictionnaire donne les expressions avec des verbes à l'infinitif. En conséquence il utilise l'adjectif possessif indéfini ***one's***.

Exemples :

find one's way	=	trouver son chemin
blow one's nose	=	se moucher
pay one's debt	=	payer ses dettes
mind one's own business	=	se mêler de ses propres affaires
put one's ideas into practice	=	mettre ses idées en pratique
ruin one's health	=	se ruiner la santé

Dans une phrase avec un verbe conjugué, *one's* sera remplacé par l'adjectif possessif approprié.

Exemple :

perdre son chemin = *lose one's way*

→ Il a perdu son chemin = *He lost **his** way.*

Traduis les phrases suivantes :

1. Je me suis mouché/e.
2. Elle a mis ses idées en pratique.
3. Il s'est ruiné la santé.
4. Occupe-toi de tes affaires!
5. Nous avons payé nos dettes.

Le dictionnaire anglais - français

1. La phonétique

La transcription phonétique figure à côté du mot, entre crochets. Elle indique la prononciation et l'accentuation des syllabes.

Attention: certains mots ayant la même orthographe se prononcent différemment selon leur sens.

Exemple :

a bow [bəʊ] = un arc

a bow [baʊ] = une révérence

Utilise le dictionnaire pour donner le sens et la nature de ces mots en te référant à la phonétique:

1. lead [led] / lead [li:d]
2. tear [teə] / tear [tɪə]
3. live [laɪv] / live [lɪv]
4. row [rəʊ] / row [raʊ]

2. Le mot de base

Il faut souvent rechercher le mot « de base » car c'est celui qui figure dans le dictionnaire.

Quand tu recherches :

- **un verbe** : pour retrouver la base verbale, il faut ignorer les terminaisons *-s*, *-es*, *-ed*, *-ing* (*take****s****, go****es****, laugh****ed****, los****ing***)
- **un nom** : il faut ignorer les marques *-s* ou *-es* du pluriel (*step****s****, box****es***)
- **un adjectif**: il faut ignorer les marques *-er* ou *-est* du comparatif et du superlatif (*high****er****, strong****est***).

NB: modifications orthographiques les plus courantes: changement du *-y* en *-ie*, redoublement de consonnes, etc ...

Quel mot rechercherais-tu si tu trouvais dans un texte les mots en gras :

1. Only the **sturdiest** trees have resisted the storm.
2. She **slammed** the door.
3. He **bullies** everyone in the school.
4. He is **sharpening** his pencil.
5. It was **damper** inside than outside.

3. Les verbes à particule

Il faut porter une attention particulière aux prépositions ou postpositions qui accompagnent certains verbes car elles en modifient le sens.

Exemples:

look ***at*** = regarder

look ***for*** = chercher

look ***after*** = s'occuper de ...

Ajoute le mot qui convient:

1. We arrived late because our car broke ...
2. She looks sad. She has just broken ... with her boyfriend.
3. Our plane took ... at 7 a.m.
4. Mr Baker is an old farmer. He hopes his son will take ... the farm.

4. Les faux amis

Certains mots, apparemment proches, n'ont cependant pas le même sens dans les deux langues.

Exemples:

librairie / *library* (= bibliothèque)

monnaie / *money* (= de l'argent)

Utilise un dictionnaire pour donner le sens de ces expressions :

1. He **passed** his exam.
2. His **exposition** was really good.
3. She writes **novels**.
4. We thought the **journey** was a bit long.

Mémento grammatical

Autres points vus au cours des unités

UNIT 1
- *both, neither*

UNIT 2
- *so, so much, so many*
- le *present perfect* avec *already* et *not yet*
- *This is the first time I have* + participe passé
- la similitude *(So / Neither do I.)* et la différence (*I do! / I don't!*)

UNIT 3
- les pronoms relatifs
- *used to; not ... any more*

UNIT 4
- le gérondif après les prépositions
- la voix passive
- *look / sound* + adjectif ; *look like / sound like* + nom

UNIT 5
- les composés en *WH-ever*
- *I'd rather ...*

UNIT 6
- le comparatif
- *how long ...? for ... / since ...*
- le *present perfect* avec *be* + *-ing*

UNIT 7
- *I wish I* + prétérit ; *I wish I* + *past perfect*

1. Les nombres

Les nombres de 1 à 12

Cardinaux (1, 2, ...)		Ordinaux (le 1er, le 2e, ...)		Cardinaux		Ordinaux	
1	one	1st	the first	7	seven	7th	the seventh
2	two	2nd	the second	8	eight	8th	the **eighth**
3	three	3rd	the third	9	nine	9th	the **ninth**
4	four	4th	the fourth	10	ten	10th	the tenth
5	five	5th	the fifth	11	eleven	11th	the eleventh
6	six	6th	the sixth	12	twelve	12th	the **twelfth**

Les nombres de 13 à 19 *(-teen)*

Cardinaux		Ordinaux	
13	**thirteen**	13th	the **thirteenth**
14	fourteen	14th	the fourteenth
15	**fifteen**	15th	the **fifteenth**
16	sixteen	16th	the sixteenth
17	seventeen	17th	the seventeenth
18	eighteen	18th	the eighteenth
19	nineteen	19th	the nineteenth

Les nombres des dizaines *(-ty)*

Cardinaux		Ordinaux	
20	**twenty**	20th	the **twentieth**
30	**thirty**	30th	the **thirtieth**
40	**forty**	40th	the **fortieth**
50	**fifty**	50th	the **fiftieth**
60	sixty	60th	the sixtieth
70	seventy	70th	the seventieth
80	eighty	80th	the eightieth
90	ninety	90th	the ninetieth

Les nombres composés : deux chiffres

Nombre des dizaines + chiffre des unités reliés par un trait d'union

Cardinaux		Ordinaux		Cardinaux		Ordinaux	
21	twenty-one	21st	the twenty-**first**	65	sixty-five	65th	the sixty-**fifth**
32	thirty-two	32nd	the thirty-**second**	76	seventy-six	76th	the seventy-sixth
43	forty-three	43rd	the forty-**third**	87	eighty-seven	87th	the eighty-seventh
54	fifty-four	54th	the fifty-fourth	98	ninety-eight	98th	the ninety-**eighth**

Les nombres à trois chiffres et plus:

100	a hundred
200	two hundred **(invariable)**
752	seven hundred **and** fifty-two
1,000	a thousand
3, 000	three thousand **(invariable)**
4, 320	four thousand, three hundred **and** twenty
500,000	five hundred thousand
1,000,000	a million
2,500,000	two and a half million **(invariable)**
1,000,000,000	(G.B.) a thousand million (U.S.) a billion

• Lorsque *hundred, thousand, million, billion* sont des **adjectifs** (numéraux), ils sont **invariables**. Ils ne se mettent donc pas au pluriel.

Exemple :

ten million inhabitants

• En revanche, lorsque ce sont des **noms**, ils peuvent se mettre au pluriel. Ils sont alors suivis de la préposition *of*.

Exemple :

des millions de gens : *millions **of** people.*

• En anglais, **la virgule** n'indique pas les décimales mais correspond en français à l'espace dans l'écriture des nombres. Elle sépare les chiffres de trois en trois.

Les nombres décimaux:

En anglais, les nombres décimaux s'écrivent avec **un point** et non une virgule.

Exemple:

4.5 (*four* ***point*** *one*) = 4,5 (quatre virgule cinq)

Les fractions:

- **Les fractions** se lisent en utilisant les nombres ordinaux
  1/10 = *one* ***tenth*** ; 1/3 = *one* ***third***

à l'exception de: 1/2 (*one* ***half***) 1/4 (***one quarter***).

- 20% se lit *twenty* ***per cent***

Les noms de souverains:

Les noms de souverains se lisent en utilisant les nombres **ordinaux**.

Exemples :

Elizabeth II = *Elizabeth* ***the Second***
Richard III = *Richard* ***the Third***

La lecture des dates:

- **Les années** jusqu'à 1999 se lisent ainsi:

Exemples:

1980 = 19 / 80 = *nineteen / eighty*
1610 = 16 / 10 = *sixteen / ten*

Lorsque la date comporte un zéro, celui-ci se lit comme **la lettre O**.

Exemple:

1802 = *eighteen O two*

A partir de l'an 2000, on lit la date comme un nombre, mais on ajoute *and* après *thousand.*

Exemple:

2003 = *two thousand and three.*

- Pour lire **les jours**, on utilise les nombres ordinaux :

Exemple:

October 23rd = the twenty-third of October ou *October the twenty-third*

2. L'heure et la durée

Expression de l'heure

one (o'clock)

one (o'clock)

one fifteen

quarter past one

one twenty-five

twenty-five past one

one thirty

half past one

one forty-five

quarter to two

one fifty

ten to two

one fifty-eight

two minutes to two*

*On ajoute le mot *minute(s)* lorsque les minutes ne sont pas un multiple de 5.

Une journée est divisée entre les heures avant midi (a.m.) et après midi (p.m.). Après midi, on reprend les heures à 1, 2, 3, etc. Ainsi, 15 h 30 se dit 3.30 (*three thirty*) ou *half past three*.

Expression de la durée

une heure (60 minutes) = *an hour*
une demi-heure = *half an hour*
une heure et demie = *an hour and a half*
deux heures = *two hours*
un quart d'heure = *a quarter of an hour*
trois quarts d'heure = *three quarters of an hour*

3. Les déterminants possessifs et les pronoms possessifs

my name	*mine*	(le mien / à moi)
your name	*yours*	(le tien / à toi)
his name	*his*	(le sien / à lui)
her name	*hers*	(le sien / à elle)
its name		
our name	*ours*	(le nôtre / à nous)
your name	*yours*	(le vôtre / à vous)
their name	*theirs*	(le leur / à eux, à elles)

4. Les pronoms personnels

Sujets	Compléments
I *live in Canada.*	*Look at* ***me****!*
You *live in Canada.*	*Look at* ***you****!*
He *lives in Canada.*	*Look at* ***him****!*
She *lives in Canada.*	*Look at* ***her****!*
It *lives in Canada.*	*Look at* ***it****!*
We *live in Canada.*	*Look at* ***us****!*
You *live in Canada.*	*Look at* ***you****!*
They *live in Canada.*	*Look at* ***them****!*

Exemples :

Does ***Bob*** *love* ***Mary****?*
↓ ↓
Does ***he*** *love* ***her****?*

Does ***Mary*** *love* ***Bob?***
↓ ↓
Does ***she*** *love* ***him****?*

Ne pas confondre :

- **les adjectifs et les formes verbales :**

your (name) et *you're (you are)*
his (name) et *he's (he is)*
their (name) et *they're (they are)*

- **les déterminants possessifs et les pronoms personnels :**

Déterminants	Pronoms
his *(name)*	***him***
our *(name)*	***us***
their *(name)*	***them***
Les **déterminants** déterminent un nom et sont donc suivis d'un nom.	Les **pronoms** remplacent un nom et ne sont pas suivis d'un nom.

5. Les pronoms réfléchis

I am looking at ***myself****.* *You are looking at* ***yourself****.*
He is looking at ***himself****.* *She is looking at* ***herself****.* *It is looking at* ***itself****.*
We are looking at ***ourselves****.* *You are looking at* ***yourselves****.* *They are looking at* ***themselves****.*

Exemples :

Bob hurt himself. = Bob hurt "Bob".
Bob s'est fait mal.
(*Bob* et *him* représentent la même personne.)

Bob hurt him. = Bob hurt a friend.
Bob lui a fait mal.
(*Bob* et *him* ne représentent pas la même personne.)

On utilise un pronom réfléchi lorsque le complément désigne la même personne que le sujet. C'est pourquoi on utilise souvent des pronoms réfléchis pour traduire des verbes pronominaux français.

Exemples:

Je me suis coupé(e). → *I cut myself.*

Nous nous sommes bien amusé(e)s. → *We enjoyed ourselves.*

Remarques:

1. Plusieurs verbes sont pronominaux en français alors qu'ils ne le sont pas en anglais.

Exemples:

He shaves. → Il se rase.
They dress. → Ils s'habillent.
She wakes up. → Elle se réveille.
I get up. → Je me lève.

2. Lorsqu'on a affaire à un verbe pronominal au pluriel en français, il faut se demander **à qui renvoie le pronom**. Il ne faut pas confondre les pronoms **réfléchis** (qui renvoient aux sujets) et les pronoms **réciproques** (qui impliquent une interaction entre deux personnes ou groupes de personnes).

Exemples :

They're looking at ***themselves****.*
Ils **se** regardent.
pronom **réfléchi** = renvoi au sujet
(chacun regarde sa propre image)

They're looking at ***each other****.*
Ils **se** regardent.
pronom **réciproque** = interaction
(chacun regarde l'autre)

6. Le génitif

• Le génitif permet d'établir des liens de relation entre des personnes et des objets (*John's book*) ou entre personnes (liens de parenté : *John's brother*). Cette relation est marquée par *'s*.

Exemples :

[*Jane*]*'s father*	[*the girl*]*'s father*	[*my best friend*]*'s father*
le père de [Jane]	le père de [la fille]	le père de [ma meilleure amie]

• Dans le cas de pluriel régulier, la marque du génitif est simplement *'*. Si le pluriel est irrégulier, on garde la marque complète *'s*.

Exemples :

[*the boys*]*' father*	[*the children*]*'s father*
le père de [les garçons] = des garçons	le père de [les enfants] = des enfants

• Attention : lorsqu'il y a un déterminant, celui-ci porte sur le premier élément.

Exemples :

[*my sister*]*'s car* = la voiture de ma sœur (ce n'est pas ma voiture).

7. Les articles the, Ø, a(n)

the	Ø	*a(n)*
• ***The*** désigne une ou des personnes, des animaux ou des objets que l'on peut identifier :	• Ø désigne toute la catégorie des personnes, des animaux ou des objets :	• ***A(n)*** désigne un élément unique :
Where's the car? (on sait de quelle voiture on parle)	*I love fast cars.* (toute la catégorie des voitures rapides, en général)	*Take a chair!* (une chaise)
Look at the lions! (on sait de quels lions on parle)	*I never drink coffee.* (le café en général)	*Give me an apple.* (une pomme)
• **Remarque :** ***The*** a la même origine que le démonstratif *this*.	• **Remarque :** Pas d'article dans les expressions telles que : - *last month* (le mois dernier) - *next year* (l'année prochaine)	• **Remarque :** Ne pas oublier l'article *a(n)* devant le nom d'un métier : *He's **a** journalist.* et devant certaines expressions : *twice **a** week; half **an** hour*

8. Les démonstratifs

This (singulier) et ***these*** (pluriel) désignent ce qui est proche de moi :

- physiquement :
  This town is really too polluted : cette ville (où je me trouve en ce moment)
  Whose are these books? (je désigne des livres qui sont près de moi)
- dans le temps :
  these last few days : ces derniers jours
  Listen to this! (je vais le dire tout de suite)

That (singulier) et ***those*** (pluriel) désignent ce qui est éloigné de moi :

- physiquement :
  That town has a nice museum : cette ville (dont je parle mais où je ne suis pas actuellement)
- dans le temps :
  in those days : à cette époque-là (éloignée du moment présent)
- dans mon appréciation :
  that stupid boy (j'ai comme un recul par rapport au garçon dont je parle)

9. L'expression d'une quantité

	noms dénombrables	**noms indénombrables**
une certaine quantité (non précisée)	***some*** *cars* / ***any*** *cars* des voitures	***some*** *time* / ***any*** *time* du temps
la totalité	***all*** *(the) cars* toutes les voitures	***all*** *the time* tout le temps
la majeure partie	***most*** *cars* la plupart des voitures	***most of*** *the time* la plupart du temps
une grande quantité	***many*** *cars* / ***a lot of*** *cars* beaucoup de voitures ***too many*** *cars* trop de voitures ***so many*** *cars* tellement de voitures	***much*** *time* / ***a lot of*** *time* beaucoup de temps ***too much*** *time* trop de temps ***so much*** *time* tellement de temps
une quantité suffisante	***enough*** *cars* assez de voitures	***enough*** *time* assez de temps
une (très) petite quantité	***(very) few*** *cars* (très) peu de voitures	***(very) little*** *time* (très) peu de temps
une quantité nulle	***no*** *cars* / ***not ... any*** *cars* pas de voitures	***no*** *time* / ***not ... any*** *time* pas de temps

10. Le comparatif et le superlatif

Adjectif de base	Comparatif de supériorité (plus ... que)	Superlatif (le plus ...)
• 1 syllabe : *small*	*smaller* **than**	**the** *smallest*
• 1 syllabe, terminé par une consonne précédée d'une voyelle : *big*	*bigger* **than**	**the** *biggest*
• 1 syllabe, terminé par ***e***: *nice*	*nicer* **than**	**the** *nicest*
• 2 syllabes, terminé en : **ow** - *narrow* ***y*** - *happy* **er** - *clever*	*narrower* **than** *happier* **than** *cleverer* **than**	**the** *narrowest* **the** *happiest* **the** *cleverest*
• 2 syllabes ou plus : *expensive*	**more** *expensive* **than**	**the most** *expensive*
• irrégulier : *good* *bad* *far*	***better than*** ***worse than*** ***further / farther than***	***the best*** ***the worst*** ***the furthest / the farthest***

	Comparatif d'égalité (aussi....que)	Comparatif d'infériorité (moins...que)
• adjectifs longs : *interesting*	**as** *interesting* **as**	**less** *interesting* **than** ou **not as** *interesting* **as**
• adjectifs courts : *tall*	**as** *tall* **as**	**not as** *tall* **as**

11. Le double comparatif

Pour exprimer une **évolution progressive**, (« de plus en plus », « de moins en moins »), on utilise le **double comparatif**.

Formation avec un adjectif

DIMINUTION		***less end less*** + adj. : *The Outback is getting less and less populated.* L'arrière-pays est de moins en moins peuplé.
ACCROISSEMENT	adjectif long	***more and more*** + adj. : *The coast is getting more and more populated.* La côte est de plus en plus peuplée.
	adjectif court	adj. + ***-er and*** adj. + ***-er*** *It's getting colder and colder.* Il fait de plus en plus froid.

Formation avec un nom

DIMINUTION	noms dénombrables	***fewer and fewer*** (comparatif de *few*) + **nom** : *There are fewer and fewer people.* Il y a de moins en moins de gens.
	noms indénombrables	***less and less*** (comparatif de *little*) + **nom :** *There is less and less wildlife.* Il y a de moins en moins d'animaux sauvages.
ACCROISSEMENT		***more and more*** (comparatif de *much* et de *many*) + **nom** : *There are more and more people.* Il y a de plus en plus de gens. *There is more and more traffic.* Il y a de plus en plus de circulation.

12. Les mots interrogatifs

Le mot interrogatif...	interroge sur...		
who	• la personne	*Who is speaking?* *Who are you talking to?*	Qui parle ? À qui parles-tu ?
whose	• le possesseur	*Whose book is this?*	À qui est ce livre ?
what	• un objet, un fait	*What are you reading?* *What happened?*	Qu'est-ce que tu lis ? Qu'est-ce qui s'est passé ?
where	• le lieu	*Where do you come from?*	D'où es-tu ?
when	• le moment	*When is your birthday?*	Quand est ton anniversaire ?
why	• la raison	*Why are you laughing?*	Pourquoi ris-tu ?
how	• la manière	*How do you go to school?*	Comment vas-tu à l'école ?

How peut être combiné à des adjectifs ou des adverbes :

how much	• la quantité	*How much money do you want?*	Combien d'argent veux-tu ?
how many	• le nombre	*How many postcards?*	Combien de cartes postales ?
how long	• la longueur (temps ou espace)	*How long will it take?* *How long is this river?*	Combien de temps cela prendra-t-il ? Quelle est la longueur de cette rivière ?
how far	• la distance	*How far is the nearest station?*	À quelle distance se trouve la gare la plus proche ?
how old	• l'âge	*How old is your brother?*	Quel âge a ton frère ?
how big	• la dimension	*How big is your garage?*	Quelle est la taille de ton garage ?
how wide	• la largeur	*How wide is the river?*	Quelle est la largeur de la rivière ?
how deep	• la profondeur	*How deep is this swimming pool?*	Quelle est la profondeur de cette piscine ?
how tall	• la taille, la hauteur	*How tall are you?*	Combien mesures-tu ?
how often	• la fréquence	*How often do you wash your hair?*	« Tous les combien » te laves-tu les cheveux ?

13. Le schéma des questions

Toute question en anglais a un schéma très régulier.

1. Si la question est totale (= on peut y répondre par *yes* ou *no*), elle commence par un auxiliaire suivi du sujet.

Exemples :

Are you ready? [*Yes, I am. / No, I'm not.*]
Will you come? [*Yes, I will. / No, I won't.*]
Do you understand? [*Yes, I do. / No, I don't.*]

En français, ces questions commencent souvent par la locution « Est-ce que » :
Est-ce que tu es prêt ? Est-ce que tu viendras ? Est-ce que tu comprends ?

2. Si la question est partielle, elle commence par un mot interrogatif suivi de l'auxiliaire et du sujet.

Exemples :

Where are you going?	Où vas-tu ?
How many brothers have you got?	Tu as combien de frères ?

3. Lorsque le mot interrogatif a la fonction de sujet, l'ordre des mots est celui d'une phrase déclarative. Comparez les exemples :

What sujet	*happened?* verbe			Qu'est-ce qui s'est passé ?
What compl.	*did* auxil.	*you* sujet	*do?* verbe	Qu'est-ce que tu as fait ?
Who sujet	*came?* verbe			Qui est venu ?
Who compl.	*did* auxil.	*you* sujet	*meet?* verbe	Qui as-tu rencontré ?
How many children sujet	*came?* verbe			Combien d'enfants sont venus ?
How many children compl.	*have* auxil.	*you* sujet	*invited?* verbe	Combien d'enfants as-tu invités ?

4. Exemples de questions :

(wh-)	auxiliaire	sujet	(verbe)	[...]
	Is	*he*		*American?*
Why	*are*	*they*	*laughing?*	
What	*were*	*you*	*doing*	*at 4.00 p.m.?*
How	*did*	*it*	*happen?*	
How much	*does*	*it*	*cost?*	
	Don't	*you*	*like*	*chocolate?*
How long	*have*	*you*	*been*	*here?*
What	*haven't*	*you*	*understood?*	
Where	*should*	*I*	*go?*	
	Will	*it*	*rain*	*tomorrow?*
How old	*can*	*she*	*be?*	
Why	*must*	*you*	*leave*	*so early?*

14. Have

Présent		Prétérit	
*I **have** (got)*	*I **haven't** (got)*	*I **had***	*I **didn't have***
*You **have** (got)*	*You **haven't** (got)*	*You **had***	*You **didn't have***
*He **has** (got)*	*He **hasn't** (got)*	*He **had***	*He **didn't have***
*She **has** (got)*	*She **hasn't** (got)*	*She **had***	*She **didn't have***
*It **has** (got)*	*It **hasn't** (got)*	*It **had***	*It **didn't have***
*We **have** (got)*	*We **haven't** (got)*	*We **had***	*We **didn't have***
*You **have** (got)*	*You **haven't** (got)*	*You **had***	*You **didn't have***
*They **have** (got)*	*They **haven't** (got)*	*They **had***	*They **didn't have***

1. Pour exprimer la possession, deux formes sont possibles : ***have got*** (uniquement au présent) ou ***have***.

Exemples :

I have got a cat. ou *I have a cat.*
J'ai un chat.

I haven't got any pens. ou *I don't have any pens.*
Je n'ai pas de stylos.

2. Pour exprimer l'obligation : *have got to* ou *have to*
Dans ce cas le verbe *have* se conjugue comme tout autre verbe : avec un auxiliaire.

Exemples :

I have got to go now. ou *I have to go now.*
Je dois partir maintenant.

When do you have to go?
Quand dois-tu partir ?

I don't have to finish it now.
Je ne suis pas obligé(e) de le finir maintenant.

3. L'auxiliaire *have / has* du *present perfect*

Exemples :

I have travelled a lot.
J'ai beaucoup voyagé.

Bob has visited a lot of countries.
Bob a visité de nombreux pays.

4. *Have* peut également être un verbe.

Exemples :

What time do you have breakfast?
À quelle heure prends-tu ton petit déjeuner ?

She is having a shower.
Elle prend une douche.

Did you have English today?
Est-ce que tu as eu un cours d'anglais aujourd'hui ?

The Wilsons are having a party.
Les Wilson organisent une soirée.

15. Be

Présent		Prétérit	
I am	*I am not*	*I was*	*I wasn't*
You are	*You aren't*	*You were*	*You weren't*
He is	*He isn't*	*He was*	*He wasn't*
She is	*She isn't*	*She was*	*She wasn't*
It is	*It isn't*	*It was*	*It wasn't*
We are	*We aren't*	*We were*	*We weren't*
You are	*You aren't*	*You were*	*You weren't*
They are	*They aren't*	*They were*	*They weren't*

1. Avec un auxiliaire de modalité, pour exprimer :

- un futur — *(It) will be / (It) won't be*
- la capacité — *(It) can be*
- l'impossibilité — *(It) can't be*
- la probabilité — *(It) must be / may be / might be*

2. Emplois spécifiques de *be*, différents de l'emploi du verbe « être » en français :

- pour exprimer un état, y compris la faim, la soif, l'âge, etc. :

Exemples :

J'ai faim. — *I am hungry.*
J'ai 13 ans. — *I am 13.*
J'ai de la chance. — *I am lucky.*

- pour traduire l'expression française « il y a » (quand elle n'est pas temporelle) :

il y a un chat / deux chats	*there is a cat / there are two cats*
il y avait une voiture / deux voitures	*there was a car / there were two cars*
il y aura un spectacle	*there will be a show*
il doit y avoir une fête	*there must be a party*

3. *Be* auxiliaire

- la forme en *-ing :*

Exemples :

What are you reading?
Que lis-tu (en ce moment) ?

What were you doing yesterday at 3.30 p.m.?
Que faisais-tu hier à 15 h 30 ?

- le passif :

Exemple :

The telephone was invented by Graham Bell.
Le téléphone a été inventé par Graham Bell.

16. La forme en *be + -ing* au présent et au prétérit

Forme affirmative	Forme négative	Forme interrogative
*I **am** / **was** working*	*I **am not** / **wasn't** working*	***Am** / **was** I working?*
*You **are** / **were** working*	*You **aren't** / **weren't** working*	***Are** / **were** you working?*
*He **is** / **was** working*	*He **isn't** / **wasn't** working*	***Is** / **was** he working?*
*She **is** / **was** working*	*She **isn't** / **wasn't** working*	***Is** / **was** she working?*
*It **is** / **was** working*	*It **isn't** / **wasn't** working*	***Is** / **was** it working?*
*We **are** / **were** working*	*We **aren't** / **weren't** working*	***Are** / **were** we working?*
*You **are** / **were** working*	*You **aren't** / **weren't** working*	***Are** / **were** you working?*
*They **are** / **were** working*	*They **aren't** / **weren't** working*	***Are** / **were** they working?*

Emploi

1. Pour commenter une action en cours de déroulement :

Exemples :

She is preparing dinner.
Elle prépare le dîner (en ce moment).

She was preparing dinner.
Elle était en train de préparer le dîner.

2. Pour exprimer une action prévue dans un avenir proche :

Exemples :

What are you doing this weekend?
Que fais-tu ce week-end ? (Quels sont tes projets ?)

3. La forme en *be + -ing* est incompatible avec des verbes qui expriment des goûts (*like, love, hate ...*) ou des processus de pensée (*want, know, remember, understand ...*).

17. Le présent

Formation

Forme affirmative	Forme négative	Forme interrogative
I work	*I don't work*	*Do I work ...?*
You work	*You don't work*	*Do you work ...?*
He works	*He doesn't work*	*Does he work ...?*
She works	*She doesn't work*	*Does she work ...?*
It works	*It doesn't work*	*Does it work ...?*
We work	*We don't work*	*Do we work ...?*
You work	*You don't work*	*Do you work ...?*
They work	*They don't work*	*Do they work ...?*

1. À la troisième personne du singulier, on ajoute un *-s* à la base verbale, à la forme affirmative.

Exemples :

He reads. *She works.*

Lorsque le verbe se termine par *-s, -x, -sh, -ch* ou par *o*, on ajoute *-es*.

Exemples :

She misses. She mixes. She washes. She watches. She goes. She does.

2. Aux formes négative et interrogative, le verbe est en base verbale et c'est l'auxiliaire qui prend la marque de la troisième personne.

Exemples :

Does she work? She doesn't work.

Emploi

Le présent simple s'emploie pour exprimer :

- des vérités générales :

  The sun rises in the east.
  Le soleil se lève à l'est.

- la permanence d'une situation :

  I live in France.
  J'habite en France.

- les habitudes ou la fréquence :

  I usually get up at 7.00.
  D'habitude, je me lève à 7 heures.

  He plays tennis twice a week.
  Il joue au tennis deux fois par semaine.

- une opinion, un goût, une volonté :

  I think, I agree, I like, I know, I remember, I want ...
  Je pense, je suis d'accord, j'aime, je sais, je me souviens, je veux ...

18. Le prétérit

Formation

Forme affirmative	Forme négative	Forme interrogative
I worked	*I didn't work*	*Did I work ...?*
You worked	*You didn't work*	*Did you work ...?*
He worked	*He didn't work*	*Did he work ...?*
She worked	*She didn't work*	*Did she work ...?*
It worked	*It didn't work*	*Did it work ...?*
We worked	*We didn't work*	*Did we work ...?*
You worked	*You didn't work*	*Did you work ...?*
They worked	*They didn't work*	*Did they work ...?*

1. À la forme affirmative, lorsque le verbe est régulier, on ajoute *-ed* ou *-d* à la base verbale.

Exemples :

I painted [ɪd]. *I worked* [t]. *I arrived* [d].

Les verbes irréguliers ont un prétérit et un participe passé qu'il faut apprendre.

Exemples :

I went (prétérit de ***go***). ***I bought*** (prétérit de ***buy***).

2. Aux formes affirmative et interrogative, le verbe est en base verbale et la marque du prétérit est dans l'auxiliaire *did*.

Exemples :

*Where **did** you go?*
Où es-tu allé(e) ?

*What **did** you buy?*
Qu'avez-vous acheté ?

*I **didn't** do anything special.*
Je n'ai rien fait de spécial.

*I **didn't** buy anything.*
Je n'ai rien acheté.

Emploi

On utilise le prétérit pour raconter un fait qui est terminé et qui n'a pas de lien avec le moment où l'on parle : un événement passé, une histoire, un conte, une biographie... Il n'y a pas nécessairement un adverbe de temps ou une date pour situer l'événement. En revanche, les adverbes ou expressions tels que ***when*** (dans un contexte passé), ***ago, last year...*** imposent un prétérit.

Exemples :

*Lindbergh **flew** across the Atlantic **in 1927**.*
Lindbergh traversa l'Atlantique en avion en 1927.

*I **went** to London with my class two years **ago**.*
Je suis allé(e) à Londres avec ma classe il y a deux ans.

Prétérit modal

• Le prétérit peut aussi ne pas avoir de valeur temporelle, mais servir à évoquer des **situations hypothétiques, imaginaires, qui n'existent pas dans la réalité.** On parle alors de « **prétérit modal** ».

Exemples :

*If I **met** Brad Pitt...*
Si je rencontrais Brad Pitt ...
(c'est bien improbable)

*If I **had** a lot of money ...*
Si j'avais beaucoup d'argent ...
(mais je n'en ai pas)

*I wish you **didn't** smoke!*
Si seulement tu ne fumais pas!
(mais tu fumes !)

• Il a la même forme que le prétérit temporel, à l'exception de ***be*** qui, au prétérit modal, devient ***were*** à toutes les personnes.

Exemples :

*If **I were** older....*
Si j'étais plus âgé(e)

*I wish **he were** here!*
Si seulement il était là !

19. Le present perfect

Formation

• Le *present perfect* est formé de l'auxiliaire ***have / has*** et du verbe au participe passé.

Forme affirmative	Forme négative	Forme interrogative
*I **have** eaten*	*I **haven't** eaten*	***Have** I eaten ...?*
*You **have** eaten*	*You **haven't** eaten*	***Have** you eaten ...?*
*He **has** eaten*	*He **hasn't** eaten*	***Has** he eaten ...?*
*She **has** eaten*	*She **hasn't** eaten*	***Has** she eaten ...?*
*It **has** eaten*	*It **hasn't** eaten*	***Has** it eaten ...?*
*We **have** eaten*	*We **haven't** eaten*	***Have** we eaten ...?*
*You **have** eaten*	*You **haven't** eaten*	***Have** you eaten ...?*
*They **have** eaten*	*They **haven't** eaten*	***Have** they eaten ...?*

• Le participe passé est identique au prétérit pour les verbes réguliers et certains verbes irréguliers :

I visited. *I have visited.*
I bought. *I have bought.*

Le participe passé a une forme qui lui est propre pour certains verbes irréguliers (*eaten, known, sung...*).

Emploi

1. Pour faire un bilan des expériences vécues

Exemples :

I have never eaten snails.
Je n'ai jamais (de ma vie) mangé d'escargots.

He has travelled a lot.
Il a beaucoup voyagé (dans sa vie).

Have you ever been to London?
Es-tu déjà allé(e) à Londres ? (au moins une fois dans ta vie)

2. Pour constater un résultat présent

Exemples :

I have lost my watch.
J'ai perdu ma montre.

The train has just left.
Le train vient de partir.

I haven't finished yet.
Je n'ai pas encore terminé.

Have you chosen your future job yet?
As-tu déjà choisi ton futur métier ?

3. Pour établir un lien entre le passé et le présent

Exemples :

I have known my best friend for two years.
Ça fait deux ans que je connais ma meilleure amie.

I have been in this class since September.
Je suis dans cette classe depuis septembre.

20. Le *past perfect*

Forme affirmative	Forme négative	Forme interrogative
*I **had** eaten*	*I **hadn't** eaten*	***Had** I eaten?*
*You **had** eaten*	*You **hadn't** eaten*	***Had** you eaten?*
*He **had** eaten*	*He **hadn't** eaten*	***Had** he eaten?*
*She **had** eaten*	*She **hadn't** eaten*	***Had** she eaten?*
*It **had** eaten*	*It **hadn't** eaten*	***Had** it eaten?*
*We **had** eaten*	*We **hadn't** eaten*	***Had** we eaten?*
*You **had** eaten*	*You **hadn't** eaten*	***Had** you eaten?*
*They **had** eaten*	*They **hadn't** eaten*	***Had** they eaten?*

Emploi

1. Pour parler d'un événement antérieur à un autre événement passé ou à une période révolue.

Exemples:

*When the bell rang, I **hadn't finished** my test.*
Quand la cloche a sonné, je n'avais pas fini mon contrôle.

*Last year, he **hadn't bought** his scooter yet.*
L'année dernière, il n'avait pas encore acheté son scooter.

2. Pour rapporter au **style indirect** des paroles au *present perfect* ou au prétérit lorsque le **verbe introducteur est au passé.**

Exemple:

*She said, "I **have** never **seen** them before."*
*She **said** she **had** never **seen** them before.*
Elle a dit qu'elle ne les avait jamais vus auparavant.

*She said, "I **saw** that show when I was in New York."*
*She **said** she **had seen** that show when she was in New York.*
Elle a dit qu'elle avait vu ce spectacle quand elle était à New York.

3. Pour évoquer des **situations hypothétiques** ou imaginaires qui n'ont pas eu lieu **dans le passé** (comme le prétérit modal évoque des situations imaginaires dans le présent).

Exemples:

*If you **had seen** him...*
Si tu l'avais vu
(mais tu ne l'as pas vu)

*If they **hadn't moved**...*
S'ils n'avaient pas déménagé
(mais ils ont déménagé)

*I wish I **had known**.*
Si seulement j'avais su !
(mais je ne savais pas)

21. Le conditionnel présent

Formation

Le conditionnel présent se forme avec l'auxiliaire ***would*** suivi de la base verbale.

Forme affirmative	Forme négative	Forme interrogative
*I **would** eat*	*I **wouldn't** eat*	***Would** I eat ...?*
*You **would** eat*	*You **wouldn't** eat*	***Would** you eat ...?*
*He **would** eat*	*He **wouldn't** eat*	***Would** he eat ...?*
*She **would** eat*	*She **wouldn't** eat*	***Would** she eat ...?*
*It **would** eat*	*It **wouldn't** eat*	***Would** it eat ...?*
*We **would** eat*	*We **wouldn't** eat*	***Would** we eat ...?*
*You **would** eat*	*You **wouldn't** eat*	***Would** you eat ...?*
*They **would** eat*	*They **wouldn't** eat*	***Would** they eat ...?*

Emploi

Lorsqu'on se place dans une situation imaginaire présente (sous-entendue ou évoquée au prétérit modal), pour dire ce qui se passerait alors.
On parle parfois « d'irréel du présent ».

Exemples :

*I'**d like** to go to Japan.*
J'aimerais aller au Japon.
(La situation imaginaire est sous-entendue : si je pouvais en décider, si j'avais les moyens...)

*If I had a lot of money, I **would travel** all over the world.*
Si j'avais beaucoup d'argent, je voyagerais partout dans le monde.
(La situation imaginaire est exprimée.)

22. Le conditionnel passé

Formation

Le conditionnel passé se forme avec l'auxiliaire ***would*** suivi de *have* + participe passé du verbe.

Forme affirmative	Forme négative	Forme interrogative
I ***would have*** *eaten*	*I* ***wouldn't have*** *eaten*	***Would*** *I* ***have*** *eaten ...?*
You ***would have*** *eaten*	*You* ***wouldn't have*** *eaten*	***Would*** *you* ***have*** *eaten ...?*
He ***would have*** *eaten*	*He* ***wouldn't have*** *eaten*	***Would*** *he* ***have*** *eaten ...?*
She ***would have*** *eaten*	*She* ***wouldn't have*** *eaten*	***Would*** *she* ***have*** *eaten ...?*
It ***would have*** *eaten*	*It* ***wouldn't have*** *eaten*	***Would*** *it* ***have*** *eaten ...?*
We ***would have*** *eaten*	*We* ***wouldn't have*** *eaten*	***Would*** *we* ***have*** *eaten ...?*
You ***would have*** *eaten*	*You* ***wouldn't have*** *eaten*	***Would*** *you* ***have*** *eaten ...?*
They ***would have*** *eaten*	*They* ***wouldn't have*** *eaten*	***Would*** *they* ***have*** *eaten ...?*

Emploi

Pour dire ce que l'on aurait fait dans une situation imaginaire passée (si le passé avait été différent de ce qu'il a été en réalité). La situation imaginaire est alors évoquée au *past perfect*. On parle parfois « d'irréel du passé ».

Exemples :

I ***would have told*** *you if you had asked me.*
Je te l'aurais dit si tu me l'avais demandé.

I ***wouldn't have known*** *what to do.*
Je n'aurais pas su quoi faire.
(La situation imaginaire n'est pas exprimée, mais sous-entendue : si je m'étais trouvé/e dans cette situation.)

23. L'expression de la possibilité et de l'obligation au conditionnel

Comme il est impossible que deux auxiliaires modaux se suivent, on ne peut pas utiliser *would* devant *can* et *must*. Il faut alors avoir recours à leurs substituts: *be able to* pour *can* et *have to* pour *must*.

Exemples :

I ***wouldn't be able to*** *see you.*
Je ne pourrais pas te voir.

I ***wouldn't have been able to*** *see you.*
Je n'aurais pas pu te voir.

I ***would have to*** *go home.*
Je serais obligé/e de rentrer chez moi.

I ***would have had to*** *go home.*
J'aurais été obligé/e de rentrer chez moi.

24. Les auxiliaires de modalité

Il n'existe que deux « temps » en anglais : le présent et le prétérit. Pour exprimer le futur ou encore des notions telles que la capacité, l'obligation, la déduction, la permission, la probabilité, etc., on emploie des auxiliaires de modalité. Voici les valeurs courantes de ces auxiliaires de modalité.

Auxiliaire	Valeur	Exemples	
will	• le futur	*It will rain tomorrow.*	Il pleuvra demain.
would	• le conditionnel	*I would help you if...* *I would have helped you if...*	Je t'aiderais si... Je t'aurais aidé si...
can / could	• la permission	*Can I watch television?*	Est-ce que je peux regarder la télévision ?
		Could I come?	Est-ce que je pourrais venir ?
	ou l'absence de permission	*No, you can't!*	Tu n'as pas le droit !
	• la capacité	*I can run very fast.* *He can read.* *We could choose.*	Je peux courir très vite. Il sait lire. On a pu choisir.
	ou l'incapacité	*I can't speak Chinese.* *I couldn't speak any more.*	Je ne sais pas parler chinois. Je ne pouvais plus parler.
	• la déduction	*She can't be here.* *It could be a bird.*	Ce n'est pas possible qu'elle soit là. Cela pourrait être un oiseau.
must	• l'obligation	*You must arrive at 8.00.*	Tu dois arriver à 8 heures.
	• l'interdiction	*You mustn't be late.*	Tu ne dois pas être en retard.
	• la déduction	*She must be ill.*	Elle doit être malade.
may / might	• la probabilité	*She may / might be ill.*	Elle est peut-être malade.
should	• le conseil	*You shouldn't eat so much.*	Tu ne devrais pas manger autant.
shall	• la suggestion	*Shall I help you?*	Veux-tu que je t'aide ?

1. Les auxiliaires de modalité ne sont pas des verbes.

- Ils n'ont pas d'infinitif.
- Ils sont suivis d'un verbe en base verbale.
- Ils ne sont jamais suivis d'un verbe en ***-ing***, ni précédés de la préposition ***to***.
- Ils ne peuvent pas être précédés d'un autre auxiliaire.

2. Les verbes équivalents des auxiliaires *can* et *must*

Puisque les auxiliaires de modalité ne peuvent être conjugués comme des verbes, on a recours à des équivalents pour exprimer les notions qu'ils recouvrent aux temps qui leur manquent.

- ***Can*** a comme équivalent ***be able (to)*** : être capable de, pouvoir.

  What will people be able to do in 2050?
  Que pourront faire les gens en 2050 ?

- ***Must*** a comme équivalent ***have to*** : avoir à, devoir.

  I will have to finish my essay before dinner.
  Il faudra que je termine ma rédaction avant le repas.

Lexique

anglais – français

français – anglais

Lexique

anglais – français

La traduction des mots donnée ici correspond à leur signification dans le contexte où ils sont utilisés dans ce manuel.

Les verbes en rouge sont des verbes irréguliers (voir la liste p. 188).

Abréviations utilisées :
n = nom, adj = adjectif, v = verbe, adv = adverbe.

A

aboard /on board	*à bord*	115
abolish	*abolir*	27
above all	*par dessus tout*	22
abroad	*à l'étranger*	69
accept	*accepter*	56
accommodation	*logement*	103
according to	*selon*	65
accurate	*précis*	115
accuse	*accuser*	56
across	*à travers*	36
actually	*en fait*	76
adapt	*s'adapter / adapter*	21
add	*ajouter*	64
advertisement	*publicité*	64
aerial	*antenne*	57
afford	*avoir les moyens*	32
afterwards	*ensuite*	44
against	*contre*	22
ages	*des années*	125
aim	*but*	115
ain't	= isn't	23
airline	*compagnie aérienne*	46
alarm system	*alarme*	64
alike	*pareil*	15
alive	*vivant*	36
all day long	*toute la journée*	48
all year round	*toute l'année*	50
allowed	*permis* (adj)	13
alone	*seul*	44
already	*déjà*	30
amazing	*étonnant*	127
among	*parmi*	13
amount	*montant, quantité*	55
amplifier	*amplificateur*	16
anger	*colère*	23
angry	*en colère*	59
another	*un autre*	32
answering machine	*répondeur téléphonique*	108
ant	*fourmi*	89
apart	*à part*	34
apartment (US)	*appartement*	33
apologize	*s'excuser*	70
appear	*apparaître*	13
appearance	*apparence*	46
area	*région*	40
argue	*se disputer*	18
arm	*bras*	28
arrow	*flèche*	46
art gallery	*musée de peinture*	47
as	*comme*	56
as a result	*le résultat, c'est que ...*	62
as early as ...	*dès*	36
as soon as	*dès que*	104
Asian	*asiatique*	34
assignment	*contrôle, examen*	124
attack (n)	*attaque*	23
attempt	*tentative*	97
attend	*assister à*	65
attract	*attirer*	34
audience	*public*	16
Aussie	*Australien*	83
award (n)	*récompense*	65
award (v)	*donner en récompense*	65
awful	*horrible*	125

B

back	*en retour*	34
back seat	*siège arrière*	48
bagful	*grande quantité*	60
bald	*chauve*	48
ban (v)	*interdire*	23
band	*groupe de musique*	13
bang (v)	*tambouriner, frapper*	24
bank (river)	*rive*	79
bathing suit	*maillot de bain*	89
beach	*plage*	51
beak	*bec*	47
bear	*ours*	49
beat	*rythme*	19
beat (v)	*battre*	60

beaver	*castor*	42
become	*devenir*	13
became → **become**		13
bee	*abeille*	89
beer	*bière*	60
begin	*commencer*	14
beginning (n)	*début*	18
behaviour	*comportement*	58
behind (**be** -)	*avoir du retard*	20
being (human -)	*être (humain)* (n)	23
belief	*croyance*	22
believe	*croire*	56
belong	*appartenir*	62
belt	*ceinture*	125
bend (n)	*tournant*	48
benefit (from)	*bénéficier (de)*	21
besides	*en dehors de*	124
bilingual	*bilingue*	49
billboard	*panneau publicitaire*	57
birth	*naissance*	55
blanket (v)	*envelopper*	123
blast (at full -)	*à plein tube, très fort*	24
bleed	*saigner*	95
blob	*grosse goutte*	126
blockbuster	*film à gros budget*	61
blood	*sang*	60
bloodshot	*injecté de sang*	113
blow	*souffler*	56
boarder	*pensionnaire*	78
boarding school	*pensionnat*	89
body	*corps*	58
bodyguard	*garde du corps*	63
boiling	*bouillant*	60
bombing	*attentat à la bombe*	97
boost	*stimuler*	51
border	*frontière*	68
bore	*ennui*	49
bored (**be** -)	*s'ennuyer*	126
boring	*ennuyeux*	23
born (**be** -)	*né*	14
borough	ici : *quartier de New York*	28
borrow	*emprunter*	70
boss	*patron*	58
both	*à la fois*	22
both of them	*eux deux*	15
both of us	*nous deux*	15
bowl	*bol, coupe*	106
brass	*cuivre*	79
break	*casser*	70
break the rules	*ne pas respecter le règlement*	34
break down	*tomber en panne*	17
break out (storm)	*exploser* (orage)	120
breath (**be** out of -)	*essoufflé*	87
bright red	*rouge vif*	50
bring up	*élever*	104
broadcast	*diffuser* (radio, TV)	78
broken → **break**	*cassé*	70
brought up→ **bring** up		104
build	*construire*	37
bulging	*plein à craquer*	125
bump (into)	*se cogner contre*	34
burn	*brûler*	48
bury	*enterrer*	79
bush	*brousse*	89
bushfire	*feu de brousse*	89

C

cab (US)	*taxi*	29
cabin	*cabane*	52
called names	*traité de tous les noms*	62
camera	*appareil photo*	55
camp counsellor	*moniteur de colonie*	44
can	*boîte de conserve*	57
can of paint	*boîte de peinture*	57
canoeing	*faire du canoë*	44
can't help (- + -ing)	*ne pas pouvoir s'empêcher (de)*	127
career	*carrière*	14
careers advisor	*conseiller d'orientation*	11
carry away	*emporter*	123
case (in -)	*au cas où*	125
cast	*ensemble des acteurs*	61
castle	*château*	72
casual	*décontracté*	75
catch up with	*rattraper (un retard)*	124
cattle	*bétail*	88
cave	*grotte*	93
cellar	*cave*	58
cement	*ciment*	64
census	*recensement*	92
channel	*chaîne (radio, TV)*	37
character	*personnage*	55
charts	*hit-parade*	23
cheap	*bon marché*	13
check	*vérifier*	64
Chinese	*chinois*	37

chorus	*refrain*	19
Christianity	*christianisme*	97
circumnavigate	*contourner*	115
citizen	*citoyen*	49
civilian	*civil* (n)	112
Civil Rights	*Droits Civiques*	22
Civil War	*Guerre de Sécession*	27
claim	*réclamer, revendiquer*	113
clap (hands)	*applaudir*	16
classical music	*musique classique*	15
classy	*élégant*	75
claw	*griffe*	47
clean (v)	*nettoyer*	44
cliff	*falaise*	98
climb	*grimper*	17
close	*près*	61
clothing	*vêtements*	102
cloudy	*couvert de nuages*	77
coast	*côte*	36
coastal	*côtier*	85
cold (n)	*froid*	115
	rhume	124
collect	*collectionner*	10
	ramasser;	86
college (US)	*premières années de faculté*	33
come a long way	*revenir de loin*	34
come to an end	*se terminer*	55
comic strip	*bande dessinée*	56
commercial	*publicité* (TV, radio)	66
common	*commun*	37
communicate	*communiquer*	46
compared to	*comparé à*	104
compete	*être en compétition*	78
complain	*se plaindre*	70
completion	*achèvement*	41
composer	*compositeur*	19
comprehensive school (GB)	*collège*	33
computer	*ordinateur*	55
computer science	*informatique*	34
computer-generated image	*image de synthèse*	60
conductor	*chef d'orchestre*	19
confide in	*se confier à*	127
confidence	*confiance*	20
constantly	*constamment*	64
contestant	*candidat*	20
continue	*continuer*	13
contrary (on the -)	*contraire (au -)*	65
convert	*convertir*	97
cope (with)	*se débrouiller (avec)*	62
copy	*exemplaire*	19
coral reef	*barrière de corail*	88
corn	*maïs (US)*	36
corridor	*couloir*	34
costume	*déguisement*	125
cotton	*coton*	13
countryside	*campagne*	107
couple (a couple of times)	*deux ou trois fois*	124
court	*tribunal*	62
crack (v)	*se fissurer*	20
crash (v)	*s'écraser*	27
crazy	*fou*	62
credits	*générique*	61
crew	*équipage*	115
criticise / -ze	*critiquer*	22
crook	*escroc*	56
crop	*récolte*	97
cross (n)	*croix*	107
crowded	*rempli de monde*	29
crude	*grossier*	23
cruise	*croisière*	32
crush	*réprimer*	97
cry	*pleurer*	45
currency	*monnaie du pays*	41
customer	*client*	67
customs	*coutumes*	36
customs	*douane*	103

D

daffodil	*jonquille*	81
daily	*quotidien*	64
dare	*oser*	70
dark	*sombre*	56
date	*un rendez-vous*	125
day-to-day	*quotidien*	13
dead end	*impasse*	113
deadly	*mortel*	91
death	*mort*	58
decrease	*diminuer*	84
deep	*profond*	120
defeat (v)	*vaincre*	27
demonstrate	*participer à une manifestation*	112
demonstration	*manifestation*	27
depend (on)	*dépendre (de)*	76
desperate	*désespéré*	64

destroy	*détruire*	27
devil-may-care	*je-m'en-foutiste*	124
diary	*journal intime*	48
different (from)	*différent (de)*	34
direct (v)	*mettre en scène*	56
director	*metteur en scène*	61
disappointed	*déçu*	20
discover	*découvrir*	20
discovery	*découverte*	82
disease	*maladie*	36
disguise	*déguisement*	56
disgust	*dégoût*	23
distance (in the -)	*au loin*	48
district	*quartier*	22
diver	*plongeur*	88
dogsled	*traîneau à chiens*	46
doorway	*entrebâillement*	122
dot	*point*	126
dot.com company	*société d'informatique*	100
downtown (US)	*centre ville*	33
drama	*théâtre*	67
draw	*dessiner*	114
drawn → **draw**		114
dress (v)	*être habillé*	75
dress (v)	*habiller*	124
drew → **draw**		115
driving licence	*permis de conduire*	89
drool	*baver d'envie*	124
drop (v)	*déposer*	127
drop (v)	*laisser tomber*	60
drought	*sécheresse*	89
drum	*tambour*	13
drummer	*batteur*	19
drums	*batterie*	19
dub	*doubler (film)*	61
dull	*inintéressant*	124
dump	*laisser tomber*	127
during	*pendant*	37
dusty	*plein de poussière*	86
Dutch	*néerlandais*	82
dwarf	*nain*	65

E

each	*chaque*	20
eagle	*aigle*	48
early (...ies)	*début des années ...*	13
early	*tôt*	48
early bird	*lève-tôt*	10
earphones	*écouteurs*	19
earring	*boucle d'oreille*	75
Easter Island	*Île de Pâques*	116
eastern	*de l'est*	37
edge (v)	*se diriger vers*	126
editing	*montage*	65
educational	*éducatif*	48
effect	*effet*	54
eject	*éliminer*	20
elevator (US)	*ascenseur*	28
eliminate	*éliminer*	20
embassy	*ambassade*	103
emigrate	*émigrer*	51
empty	*vide*	57
encounter	*rencontrer*	105
encourage	*encourager*	22
end up	*finir*	18
endangered	*en voie de disparition*	47
ending	*fin*	18
engineer	*ingénieur*	104
enjoy	*aimer, apprécier*	10
enough	*assez*	20
equal	*égal*	36
erase	*effacer*	57
escape	*échapper à*	51
especially	*particulièrement*	22
even	*même*	34
even though	*même si*	90
event	*événement*	36
everything	*tout*	48
evil	*méchant, mal*	120
evolve	*évoluer*	13
except	*sauf*	36
excited	*très content, passionné*	48
exclusive	*privilégié*	62
exhausted	*épuisé*	87
expect	*s'attendre à*	20
expectancy (life -)	*espérance (de vie)*	92
expenses	*dépenses*	79
explorer	*explorateur*	43
export	*exporter*	84
express	*exprimer*	13
extinct	*disparu*	47
extra	*figurant*	61
extremely	*extrêmement*	23

Lexique

F

fail	*être insuffisant*	97
faint	*s'évanouir*	17
faithful	*fidèle*	79
fake (n)	*imposteur*	56
fake (adj)	*faux*	56
fame	*renommée*	62
famous	*célèbre*	13
fan	*fan*	63
fan	*ventilateur*	60
far and wide	*dans tous les coins*	48
farmer	*fermier*	83
fashion	*mode*	76
fashion (out of -)	*démodé*	75
fashion designer	*couturier*	75
favourite	*préféré*	46
feast	*fête*	36
feather	*plume*	47
feed (on)	*se nourrir (de)*	50
feel	*se sentir*	20
feeling	*sentiment*	13
fees	*frais à payer*	79
fence (v)	*clôturer*	64
few (adj)	*quelques*	21
few	*peu de*	83
field	*champ*	32
fierce	*très violent*	116
fight	*se battre*	22
figure	*silhouette*	120
finish	*finir*	34
fire	*feu*	69
fire (at) (v)	*faire feu (sur)*	112
first	*premièrement*	34
fish (v)	*pêcher*	50
fishing license	*permis de pêche*	105
fishing rod	*canne à pêche*	89
fist	*poing*	64
fit	*en forme*	20
flag	*drapeau*	41
flat (GB)	*appartement*	33
flea	*puce*	76
flight	*vol (avion)*	85
floatplane	*hydravion*	46
floaty	*ample*	125
flock (v)	*affluer*	64
flooded	*inondé*	86
floor	*étage*	28
flour	*farine*	60
flow	*couler*	78
fluently	*couramment*	109
fly	*voler*	30
fog	*brouillard*	60
follow around	*poursuivre*	63
footprint	*empreinte de pied*	64
forbid	*interdire*	97
forbidden → **forbid**		97
foreign	*étranger* (adj)	46
foreigner	*étranger* (n)	103
forever	*pour toujours*	18
form (GB)	*classe*	33
formal dress	*tenue habillée*	75
former	*ancien*	69
found	*fonder*	36
free	*libre*	83
free period	*heure libre entre les cours*	108
freedom	*liberté*	26
freeze	*geler*	115
froze → **freeze**		115
friendly	*sympathique*	70
frightful	*effroyable*	47
from all over	*de partout*	34
fruitful	*profitable*	126
full	*repu, rassasié*	70
full-size	*grandeur nature*	65
full works	*la totale*	124
fun	*drôle*	48
funeral	*enterrement*	81
fur	*fourrure*	40
further	*plus loin*	92
fuss (**make** a -)	*histoires (faire des -)*	76

G

gamble	*jouer; parier*	30
gas (US)	*essence*	33
gather	*rassembler*	88
GCSE (General Certificate of Secondary Education	*équivalent du Brevet des Collèges*	124
gear	*attirail*	125
gentle	*doux, gentil*	56
Germany	*Allemagne*	37
get (to)	*se rendre à, aller à*	28
get around	*se déplacer*	51
get bored with	*s'ennuyer*	18

get close (to)	*s'appprocher*	63
get exercise	*faire du sport*	50
get on	*s'entendre*	18
get rid of	*se débarasser de*	58
get through	*endurer*	20
giant	*géant*	64
gift	*cadeau*	126
glass	*verre*	51
global warming	*réchauffement de la planète*	85
glove	*gant*	125
glue	*colle*	125
go for	*choisir*	125
go on	*se passer*	16
go out (light)	*s'éteindre*	17
goal	*but*	122
gold digger	*chercheur d'or*	83
Gold Rush	*Ruée vers l'Or*	37
golden	*d'or*	55
gorgeous	*sublime*	124
grade (US)	*classe*	33
grass	*herbe*	89
grease	*graisse*	87
greatly	*beaucoup*	83
Greek	*grec*	37
grew up → **grow** up		104
grin	*sourire*	122
grow up	*grandir*	14
guided tour	*visite guidée*	47
gun	*revolver, fusil*	35
guts (**have** the - to)	*avoir le cran de*	127

H

haircut	*coupe de cheveux*	75
half (of)	*moitié*	35
hammer and tongs	*avec violence*	124
handbag	*sac à main*	75
handprint	*empreinte de main*	64
hang	*accrocher*	44
happen	*se passer*	16
harassment	*harcèlement*	103
hard	*dur*	20
hardly	*à peine*	127
harmless	*inoffensif*	91
harsh	*rude*	51
harvest	*moisson, récolte*	36
hatred	*haine*	112
haunted	*hanté*	59
head (v)	*aller vers*	116
head start	*longueur d'avance*	124
head teacher (GB)	*principal de collège*	33
headache	*mal à la tête*	102
health	*santé*	92
hear	*entendre*	20
heard → **hear**		20
heart	*coeur*	20
heed	*faire attention à*	113
height	*hauteur*	28
heights (**be** afraid of -)	*avoir le vertige*	51
hesitate	*hésiter*	34
hidden → **hide**		56
hide	*cacher*	70
hijacked	*détourné par des pirates de l'air*	27
hike	*faire une randonnée*	30
hire	*louer, embaucher*	58
Hispanic	*latino-américain*	23
Holy Ghost	*Saint Esprit*	106
homeless	*sans abri*	47
homesick	*qui s'ennuie de chez lui*	20
hope (n)	*espoir*	13
hope (v)	*espérer*	26
host family	*famille d'accueil*	70
housing estate	*programme immobillier*	64
howl	*hurler*	122
hug	*prendre dans ses bras*	127
huge	*immense*	51
hunger strike	*grève de la faim*	112
hunt	*chasser*	46
hurricane	*ouragan*	56

I

ice cream	*crème glacée*	60
ice rink	*patinoire*	51
ice pack	*bloc de glace*	116
icy (road)	*verglacé*	49
ignore	*ne pas s'occuper de*	70
illuminate	*enluminer*	107
impressive	*impressionnant*	93
immune	*protégé*	113
imprint	*empreinte*	64

improve (on)	*améliorer*	55
improvise	*improviser*	55
in (**be** -)	*être à la maison*	124
include	*inclure*	13
including	*y compris*	34
increase (v)	*augmenter*	51
indoor	*couvert*	51
indoors	*à l'intérieur*	50
inhabitant	*habitant*	28
inherit	*hériter*	107
inside	*à l'intérieur*	28
instance (for -)	*exemple (par -)*	62
instant (adj)	*instantané*	50
instead of	*au lieu de*	106
instructor	*moniteur*	52
introduce	*(se) présenter*	11
introduce	*introduire*	22
invade	*envahir, entrer dans*	62
invader	*envahisseur*	68
Irish	*irlandais*	97
Italian	*italien*	37

J

Japanese	*japonais*	27
jealousy	*jalousie*	20
Jew	*Juif*	37
join	*joindre, relier*	41
journey	*voyage*	115

K

keep + ing	*ne pas cesser de*	70
key	*clef*	58
keyboard	*clavier*	19
kid	*gamin*	34
kind (adj)	*gentil*	120
kind (n)	*sorte*	13
kindness	*gentillesse*	61
knee	*genou*	126
knock	*frapper*	56

L

labourer	*ouvrier agricole*	114
lace	*dentelle*	125
lack of	*manque de*	115
lacy	*en dentelle*	125
land (n)	*terre*	36
landmark	*lieu connu*	64
landscape	*paysage*	55
language	*langue*	13
lap (**fall** into one's -)	*tomber du ciel*	124
large (city)	*grand*	51
last (adj)	*dernier*	37
last (v)	*durer*	55
last but not least	*le dernier mais non le moindre*	50
late ...	*fin des années ...*	22
late	*tard*	44
laugh	*rire*	45
law	*loi*	35
lawyer	*avocat*	100
lead	*conduire, mener*	36
leading actor	*acteur principal*	65
leading role	*rôle principal*	58
leaf / leaves	*feuille/s*	89
leather	*cuir*	75
leave	*quitter*	18
lecture	*leçon de morale*	125
led → **lead**	*conduire*	36
left → **leave**		37
left	*qui reste*	70
left-handed	*gaucher*	103
lend	*prêter*	25
length	*longueur*	28
let	*laisser; autoriser*	44
level	*niveau*	92
librarian	*bibliothécaire*	65
lie	*être allongé*	24
life	*vie*	23
life jacket	*gilet de sauvetage*	44
lift (GB)	*ascenseur*	33
light (v)	*allumer*	83
light (n)	*lumière*	46
light bulb	*ampoule électrique*	46
light up	*éclairer*	50
lighting	*éclairage*	79
lightning	*foudre*	93
link (v)	*relier*	37
little (very-)	*peu (trés-)*	21
live (adj)	*en direct*	20
lively	*vivant, plein de vie*	97
loads of	*beaucoup de*	76
locate	*situer*	34
loneliness	*solitude*	13
long-lost	*perdu de vue*	56
look	*avoir l'air*	59

look forward to	*attendre avec impatience*	124
look like	*ressembler à*	60
look up	*lever les yeux*	121
loose	*pas serré*	75
lorry (GB)	*camion*	33
lose face	*perdre la face*	34
loud	*haut (son)*	19
low	*bas (son)*	19
luck	*chance*	124
lying → **lie**		121
lyrics	*paroles de chanson*	19

M

magician	*illusionniste*	55
magnet	*aimant; qui attire*	34
mainly	*principalement*	37
make a fire	*faire du feu*	44
make it (not-)	*foirer, rater*	125
mammal	*mammifère*	89
manage	*arriver à*	62
manipulate	*manipuler*	60
mansion	*grande demeure*	56
map	*carte*	102
maple tree	*érable*	42
march (v)	*défiler*	112
mashed potatoes	*purée de pommes de terre*	60
mask	*masque*	60
mast	*mât*	118
masterpiece	*chef d'oeuvre*	61
mean	*vouloir dire*	34
melting pot	*creuset*	36
memento	*souvenir*	64
mike	*micro*	19
mind	*être égal*	70
I don't mind (v)	*Ça m'est égal*	
mine	*à moi*	16
miss (v)	*rater*	122
miss (v)	*manquer*	20
I miss you	*Tu me manques*	
mix (v)	*(se) mélanger*	36
moan (v)	*ronchonner*	70
mock	*faux; parodie de*	56
monastery	*monastère*	97
monk	*moine*	107
monsoon	*mousson*	83
mood (be in the - for)	*avoir envie de*	76
mosquito	*moustique*	89
most	*la plupart*	20
mostly	*principalement*	37
mother tongue	*langue maternelle*	35
motion	*mouvement*	55
motionless	*immobile*	48
motorway (GB)	*autoroute*	33
mountain	*montagne*	55
move	*bouger*	48
movie (US)	*film*	61
museum	*musée*	29
musical instrument	*instrument de musique*	14
musician	*musicien*	13
mysterious	*mystérieux*	58

N

naff	*« moche »*	75
name (brand-)	*marque*	75
nasty	*méchant*	56
national holiday	*jour(s) férié(s)*	36
native (adj)	*natal*	13
neck	*cou*	122
need (v)	*avoir besoin de*	20
need (n)	*besoin*	104
neighbour	*voisin*	42
neighbourhood	*voisinage, quartier*	23
neither of us	*aucun de nous*	15
nerve-racking	*éprouvant pour les nerfs*	21
nest	*nid*	47
Netherlands (the -)	*les Pays-Bas*	37
New Deal	*Nouvelle Donne*	27
newcomer	*nouveau*	103
news (the -)	*les informations*	113
nickname	*surnom*	65
night owl	*couche-tard*	10
no sooner ... than	*à peine ... que*	124
Nobel Prize	*prix Nobel*	107
noise	*bruit*	29
noisy	*bruyant*	79
north	*nord*	27
Northern	*du nord*	50
nose	*nez*	28
not anywhere	*nulle part*	48
not at all	*pas du tout*	20
notice	*remarquer*	76
novel	*roman*	52
nowadays	*de nos jours, actuellement*	97

O

obvious	*évident*	120
off (**be** -)	*partir, être lancé*	124
oil	*huile*	46
old-fashioned	*démodé*	103
Olympic Games	*jeux olympiques*	83
once again	*encore une fois*	121
onwards (from ... -)	*à partir de ...*	68
opening	*ouverture*	83
open-minded	à *l'esprit ouvert*	103
opportunity	*occasion*	99
orchestra	*orchestre classique*	19
other	*autre*	20
out (**be** -)	*ne pas être à la maison*	124
outside	*dehors*	46
overweight	*trop gros*	62
overwhelmed	*accablé*	116
own (adj)	*à soi*	14
owner	*propriétaire*	92

P

packed (day)	*chargé*	20
paddle	*pagayer*	48
pain	*douleur*	122
painful	*douloureux*	34
painting	*tableau (peinture)*	79
pancake	*crêpe*	52
part	*rôle*	61
part of (**be**-)	*partie de (faire-)*	34
past (in the -)	*passé (dans le passé)*	46
pavement (GB)	*trottoir*	33
peaceful	*pacifique*	97
peasant	*paysan*	97
peel	*éplucher*	95
performer	*artiste de scène*	19
period	*heure de cours*	108
petrol (GB)	*essence*	33
phrase	*expression*	65
pick	*ramasser; cueillir*	13
piece	*morceau*	70
pier	*jetée (bord de mer)*	79
pinched (look -)	*avoir les traits tirés*	124
place	*endroit*	30
plan (v)	*projeter de*	32
play (n)	*pièce de théâtre*	79
plot	*complot*	48
plug	*prise électrique*	102
point out	*faire remarquer*	124
poisonous	*vénéneux*	90
polluted	*pollué*	49
pond	*étang*	126
poney-trekking	*randonnée à dos de poney*	10
populated	*peuplé*	35
Portuguese	*portugais*	82
pound (v)	*battre fort*	20
poverty level	*seuil de pauvreté*	35
power	*puissance*	69
prejudice	*préjugé*	103
presumably	*sans doute*	125
pretend	*faire semblant de*	70
prevent (from + -ing)	*empêcher (de)*	64
price	*prix*	28
privacy	*vie privée; intimité*	62
private	*privé*	62
process (v)	*traiter*	67
produce	*produire*	55
producer	*producteur*	55
programme	*émission*	20
protected	*protégé*	49
protest	*protestation*	22
pull off	*arracher*	121
puppet	*marionnette*	60
push the point	*insister*	126
put out a fire	*éteindre un feu*	44
put up with	*supporter*	48
puzzled	*étonné*	59

Q

queue (v)	*faire la queue*	77
quietly	*tranquillement*	24

R

radio-controlled	*télécommandé*	60
rag	*chiffon*	125
raid (v)	*mettre à sac*	97
	faire un raid	125
railroad (US)	*chemin de fer*	37
railway (GB)	*chemin de fer*	41
rainforest	*forêt tropicale*	89
raise	*lever*	48
range from ... to (v)	*aller de ... à*	65
rate	*taux*	92
rather (would -)	*préférer*	72
rattlesnake	*serpent à sonnette*	30

raw	*cru*	52
ray	*rayon*	115
react	*réagir*	23
reason	*raison*	37
rebel (v)	*se rebeller*	23
recipe	*recette*	70
recognize / -se	*reconnaître*	58
record (n)	*disque*	19
record (v)	*enregistrer*	16
recording	*enregistrement*	19
reflect	*refléter*	22
refugee	*réfugié*	37
regret (v)	*regretter*	20
rehearsal	*répétition*	20
reign	*règne*	69
reject	*rejeter*	22
relief	*soulagement*	125
religious	*religieux*	36
remain	*rester*	97
remove	*enlever*	57
rent (v)	*louer*	51
request (v)	*prier qqn de*	67
research (n)	*recherche*	100
reservation	*réserve*	36
resort	*station (touristique)*	47
reveal	*révéler*	58
rhythm	*rythme*	19
ribbon	*ruban*	106
rifle	*fusil*	46
right (n)	*droit (n)*	22
right (adj)	*juste*	48
riot	*émeute*	97
rip off	*arracher*	17
rise	*se lever* (soleil)	10
road sign	*panneau routier*	107
rock-climbing	*escalade*	10
Rockies (the -)	*les Rocheuses*	30
role	*rôle*	58
roof	*toit*	79
rotten day	*sale journée*	124
row	*ramer*	72
rubber	*caoutchouc*	60
rubbish (n)	*nul, sans intérêt*	126
rule	*règlement*	34
run (a pub)	*tenir (un café)*	104
run away	*s'échapper en courant*	122
running	*d'affilée*	124
rush out	*sortir précipitamment*	119
Russian	*russe*	37
rusty	*rouillé*	104

S

sad	*triste*	18
sadness	*tristesse*	120
safe (n)	*coffre-fort*	58
sail	*naviguer*	36
sailor	*marin*	69
sales	*soldes*	126
salmon	*saumon*	99
salt	*sel*	49
sand	*sable*	49
sang → **sing**		13
satellite dish	*antenne parabolique*	57
sauerkraut	*choucroute*	115
savannah	*savane*	83
scatter	*éparpiller*	48
Scottish	*écossais*	68
scream	*hurler*	16
screen	*écran*	61
scrub	*brousse*	83
scurvy	*scorbut*	115
seal	*phoque*	50
search for	*aller à la recherche de*	122
seasick (**be** -)	*avoir le mal de mer*	102
seaside	*bord de mer*	99
second-hand	*d'occasion*	76
seem	*sembler*	48
selfish	*égoïste*	25
send	*envoyer*	18
sent → **send**		58
session	*séance*	20
set (n)	*plateau de tournage*	61
settle	*s'installer*	37
settler	*colon*	26
several	*plusieurs*	20
shadow	*ombre*	122
shamrock	*trèfle*	106
shape (v)	*constituer, former*	42
shape (n)	*forme*	76
shark	*requin*	89
sharp	*pointu*	53
sheep	*mouton(s)*	84
ship (n)	*bateau*	36
ship (v)	*envoyer en bateau*	82
shoot	*tourner un film;*	55
	tirer (arme à feu)	112
shooting	*tournage*	62
shopkeeper	*commerçant*	83
shopping mall	*centre commercial*	51
shot → **shoot**		

shot (n)	*prise de vue*	61
shoulder	*épaule*	127
shout	*crier*	87
show (v)	*montrer*	20
show (n)	*spectacle*	20
shower	*douche*	58
shown → **show**		58
shuttle	*navette*	81
sidewalk (US)	*trottoir*	33
sight	*spectacle*	76
sighting	*chose vue*	48
sightseeing (**go**-)	*faire du tourisme*	47
sign (n)	*signe*	34
	panneau	57
silk	*soie*	75
silver	*argent*	23
simmer (down)	*se calmer*	48
sing	*chanter*	13
size	*taille*	58
skin	*peau*	91
skip	*ne pas aller à*	126
skyscraper	*gratte-ciel*	27
slave	*esclave*	13
slavery	*esclavage*	13
sleepy (**feel**-)	*avoir envie de dormir*	45
slide	*toboggan*	51
smell (n)	*odeur*	95
smile	*sourire*	18
snake	*serpent*	90
snorkelling	*plongée* (avec un tuba)	10
snow	*neige*	60
Snow White	*Blanche Neige*	67
soccer	*football*	106
soft	*doux*	61
soft drink	*boisson non alcoolisée*	46
softness	*douceur*	61
soil	*sol*	49
soldier	*soldat*	82
song	*chanson*	13
sound (n)	*son*	13
sound (v)	*avoir l'air*	59
sound like	*ressembler à*	60
South	*sud*	13
southern	*du sud*	13
space shuttle	*navette spatiale*	81
Spanish	*espagnol*	37
sparsely	*peu peuplé*	83
species	*espèce*	47
spend	*passer*	48
spices	*épices*	79
spicy	*épicé*	32
spider	*araignée*	90
spooky	*qui donne la chair de poule*	59
spot (v)	*apercevoir*	125
spotlight	*projecteur*	17
spread	*étaler*	58
stab	*poignarder*	58
staff	*personnel* (n)	104
stage	*scène*	16
stain	*tache*	87
stairs	*escalier*	58
staircase	*escalier*	122
stall	*étalage*	125
stare	*regarder fixement*	48
start	*commencer*	18
starvation	*faim; famine*	97
state	*état*	13
stay	*rester*	20
steal	*voler, dérober*	58
steam off	*foncer sur*	126
step	*marche*	28
stick	*coller; rester collé*	65
stick insect	*phasme*	62
stinking	*épouvantable*	124
stock market	*bourse*	27
stomp off	*partir bruyamment*	124
stone	*pierre*	120
store	*magasin*	51
stormy	*orageux*	56
story	*histoire*	23
storytelling	*conte*	13
straight face (**keep** a -)	*garder son sérieux*	125
strange	*étrange*	58
strangle	*étrangler*	118
strewn	*éparpillé*	113
strict	*sévère*	20
strong	*fort*	20
struggle	*lutte*	22
stuck→ **stick**		65
studies	*études*	34
study	*étudier*	14
stuff	*trucs*	125
stylish	*élégant*	75
subtitle	*sous-titre*	61
subway (US)	*métro*	33
succeed	*réussir*	34
successful	*qui a du succès*	47
such as	*tel que*	13
sucked (into)	*aspiré*	62

suffer from	*souffrir de*	23
sugar cane	*canne à sucre*	13
suit (v)	*aller, convenir*	75
summer camp	*colonie de vacances*	44
sun-bathe	*se faire bronzer*	87
sunlight	*ensoleillement*	55
sunset	*coucher de soleil*	93
sun-tanned	*bronzé*	86
support	*soutenir*	20
surrounded	*entouré*	51
survive	*survivre*	36
suspect (v)	*soupçonner*	58
suspension	*renvoi*	34
sweat (v)	*transpirer*	20
syrup	*sirop*	60

T

tabloid	*journal populaire*	62
tail	*queue* (animal)	47
take (sbdy to)	*emmener; prendre*	56
take cover	*se mettre à l'abri*	48
take place	*avoir lieu*	41
talkie	*film parlant*	55
tan	*bronzage*	87
tatty	*usagé, défraîchi*	125
tear (n)	*larme*	113
tedious	*ennuyeux*	115
terrific	*génial*	20
terrified	*terrifié*	59
thanks to	*grâce à*	20
thick	*épais*	61
thickness	*épaisseur*	61
thin	*mince*	62
thirdly	*troisièmement*	34
thirds (two -)	*tiers (deux -)*	51
though	*mais*	126
thousands (of)	*des milliers (de)*	93
threaten	*menacer*	34
threw → **throw**		
thriller	*film à suspense*	58
thrilling	*excitant*	20
through	*à travers, par*	23
throughout	*partout dans*	23
throw	*jeter; lancer*	79
tie (n)	*lien*	69
title	*titre*	114
tight	*serré*	75
tight-fitting	*moulant*	75
time (at the same -)	*temps (en même -)*	16
tin	*fer blanc*	106
tin whistle	*flûte*	106
tobacco	*tabac*	36
together	*ensemble*	44
top	*sommet*	28
torn apart	*séparé (de force)*	113
touch (v)	*toucher*	34
touch (n)	*touche, note*	76
tough	*dur, violent*	34
tour (**go** on -)	*tournée (faire une -)*	20
tourist site	*lieu touristique*	51
towards	*vers, envers*	55
trade (n)	*commerce*	40
trader	*marchand*	69
traffic	*circulation*	29
traffic lights	*feux de circulation*	57
trained	*formé, qualifié*	104
training	*formation*	20
transaction	*opération (en banque)*	67
transport (v)	*déporter*	82
transportation	*transport*	46
travel	*voyager*	32
treasure	*trésor*	56
tremble	*trembler*	20
trench	*tranchée*	113
trendy	*à la mode*	75
trial	*procès, jugement*	112
tribe	*tribu*	36
trick	*astuce*	60
trip	*voyage*	26
trouble	*problème*	13
truck (US)	*camion*	33
true	*vrai*	32
trunk	*tronc*	89
trust	*faire confiance à*	56
tune	*air, mélodie*	19
turning point	*tournant*	58
typhoon	*typhon*	89

U

underground (n) (GB)	*métro*	33
underground (adj)	*souterrain*	49
unemployment	*chômage*	23
unfortunately	*malheureusement*	20
unless	*sauf si*	104
until	*jusqu'à*	37
unusual	*inhabituel*	77

upset	*contrarié*	48
use	*utiliser*	13
useful	*utile*	52
usually	*habituellement*	21

V

vacation (US)	*vacances*	32
valuables	*objets de valeur*	67
Vietnamese	*vietnamien*	83
view	*vue*	29
viewer	*télé/spectateur*	20
violin	*violon*	19
vocal class	*cours de chant*	20
vote (n)	*vote*	20
vote (v)	*voter*	20
voyage	*voyage en mer*	115

W

wages	*salaire*	79
wall	*mur*	68
war	*guerre*	27
washboard	*planche à laver*	13
wasp	*guêpe*	89
waterfall	*chute d'eau*	55
Waterlilies	*Nymphéas*	126
waterproof	*imperméable (adj.)*	102
waterskiing (**go**-)	*faire du ski nautique*	10
wave (n)	*vague*	37
way	*façon*	23
	chemin	34
way of life	*mode de vie*	22
way with (**have** a -)	*savoir manier*	107
weak	*faible*	85
wealthy	*aisé, riche*	51
weapon	*arme*	34
wedding	*mariage*	81
weight	*poids*	28
West Indies (the-)	*les Antilles*	97
wet	*mouillé, humide*	64
whale	*baleine*	48
whatever	*quoi que*	74
whenever	*chaque fois que*	74
whereas	*tandis que*	20
wherever	*partout où*	74
whether	*si oui ou non*	125
while	*pendant que*	13
whoever	*quiconque*	74
wild	*sauvage*	44
wildlife	*faune et flore*	47
will	*volonté*	20
wimp	*mauviette*	124
win	*gagner*	20
wind	*vent*	29
windsurfing (**go**-)	*faire de la planche à voile*	10
wine	*vin*	84
wine-grower	*viticulteur*	85
winner	*gagnant*	65
wipe	*essuyer*	113
wire	*fil électrique*	119
witch	*sorcière*	67
without	*sans*	51
wobbly	*tremblant*	126
wonder (no-)	*pas étonnant*	62
wonder (v)	*se demander*	71
wood	*bois*	52
wool / woolen	*laine / en laine*	75
word	*mot*	19
work out	*comprendre*	124
workout	*entraînement physique*	20
work permit	*permis de travail*	103
world	*monde*	34
World Fair	*Foire Internationale*	41
worse	*pire*	76
wrinkled	*ridé*	118

Y

yell	*crier*	48
yet (not-)	*pas encore*	98
yet	*pourtant*	34
youth hostel	*auberge de jeunesse*	32

Z

zipper	*fermeture éclair*	51

français – anglais

Abréviations utilisées :
n = nom, adj = adjectif, v = verbe,
adv = adverbe.

A

à la mode	*trendy*	75
à l'étranger	*abroad*	69
à l'intérieur	*inside*	28
à moi	*mine*	16
à part	*apart*	34
à soi	*own*	14
à travers	*across*	36
à travers, par	*through*	23
abolir	*abolish*	27
accepter	*accept*	56
accrocher	***hang***	44
accuser	*accuse*	56
acteur principal	*leading actor*	65
actuellement	*nowadays*	97
aigle	*eagle*	48
aimer, apprécier	*enjoy*	10
air (musique)	*tune*	19
aisé, riche	*wealthy*	51
alarme	*alarm system*	64
Allemagne	*Germany*	37
allumer	***light*** (v)	83
ambassade	*embassy*	103
améliorer	*improve (on)*	55
amplificateur	*amplifier*	16
ampoule électrique	*light bulb*	46
ancien	*former*	69
antenne	*aerial*	57
antenne parabolique	*satellite dish*	57
Antilles	*West Indies (the -)*	97
apparaître	*appear*	13
appareil photo	*camera*	55
apparence	*appearance*	46
appartement	*flat* (GB) ; *apartment* (US)	33
appartenir à	*belong to*	62
applaudir	*clap (hands)*	16
araignée	*spider*	90
argent	*silver*	23
arme	*weapon*	34
arracher	*rip off*	16
arriver à	*manage*	62
artiste de scène	*performer*	19
ascenseur	*lift* (GB);	33
	elevator (US)	28
asiatique	*Asian*	34
assez	*enough*	20
assister à	*attend*	65
astuce	*trick*	60
attaque	*attack* (n)	23
attirer	*attract*	34
au lieu de	*instead of*	106
au loin	*distance (in the -)*	48
auberge de jeunesse	*youth hostel*	32
aucun de nous	*neither of us*	15
augmenter	*increase*	51
autoroute	*motorway* (GB);	33
	highway (US)	33
autre (un-)	*another*	20
avocat	*lawyer*	100
avoir besoin de	*need*	20
avoir du retard	***be*** *behind*	20
avoir envie de	***be*** *in the mood for*	76
avoir envie de dormir	***feel*** *sleepy*	45
avoir l'air	*look*	59
	sound	59
avoir le mal de mer	***be*** *seasick*	102
avoir le vertige	***be*** *afraid of heights*	51
avoir les moyens	*afford*	32
avoir lieu	***take*** *place*	41

B

baleine	*whale*	48
bande dessinée	*comic strip*	56
barrière de corail	*coral reef*	88
bas (son)	*low*	19
bateau	*ship*	36
batterie	*drums*	19
batteur	*drummer*	19
battre fort	***beat*** (v)	20
beaucoup de	*loads of*	76

Lexique

bec	*beak*	47
bénéficier (de)	*benefit (from)*	21
besoin (avoir -)	*need*	20
besoin	*need*	104
bétail	*cattle*	88
bibliothécaire	*librarian*	65
bière	*beer*	60
bilingue	*bilingual*	49
bois	*wood*	52
boîte de conserve	*can*	57
boîte de peinture	*can of paint*	57
bol, coupe	*bowl*	106
bon marché	*cheap*	13
bord de mer	*seaside*	99
boucle d'oreille	*earring*	75
bouger	*move*	48
bouillant	*boiling*	60
bras	*arm*	28
bronzage	*tan*	87
bronzé	*sun-tanned*	86
brouillard	*fog*	60
brousse	*bush*	89
bruit	*noise*	29
brûler	*burn*	48
bruyant	*noisy*	79

C

cabane	*cabin*	52
cacher	***hide***	56
camion	*lorry* (GB); *truck* (US)	33 33
campagne	*countryside*	107
candidat	*contestant*	20
canne à pêche	*fishing rod*	89
canne à sucre	*sugar cane*	13
caoutchouc	*rubber*	60
carrière	*career*	14
carte	*map*	102
castor	*beaver*	42
cave	*cellar*	58
célèbre	*famous*	13
centre commercial	*shopping mall*	51
centre ville	*downtown* (US) *towncenter* (GB)	33
chaîne (radio, TV)	*channel*	37
champ	*field*	32
chanson	*song*	13
chaque	*each*	20
chasser	*hunt*	46
château	*castle*	72
chef d'œuvre	*masterpiece*	61
chef d'orchestre	*conductor*	19
chemin de fer	*railway* (GB); *railroad* (US)	41 37
chercheur d'or	*gold digger*	83
chinois	*Chinese*	37
chômage	*unemployment*	23
christianisme	*Christianity*	97
ciment	*cement*	64
circulation	*traffic*	29
citoyen	*citizen*	49
classe	*form* (GB); *grade* (US)	33 33
clavier	*keyboard*	19
clef	*key*	58
client	*customer*	67
cœur	*heart*	20
coffre-fort	*safe*	58
colère	*anger*	23
en colère	*angry*	23
collectionner	*collect*	59
collège	*comprehensive school* (GB)	33
coller, rester collé	***stick***	65
colon	*settler*	26
colonie	*summer camp*	44
comme	*as*	56
commencer	*begin* *start*	14 18
commerçant	*shopkeeper*	83
commerce	*trade* (n)	40
commun	*common*	37
communiquer	*communicate*	46
compagnie aérienne	*airline*	46
comparé à	*compared to*	104
complot	*plot*	48
comportement	*behaviour*	58
compositeur	*composer*	19
conduire, mener	***lead***	36
confiance	*confidence*	20
conseiller d'orientation	*careers adviser*	11
constamment	*constantly*	64
constituer, former	*shape*	42
construire	***build***	37
continuer	*continue*	13

contraire (au -)	*contrary (on the -)*	66
contrarié	*upset*	48
contre	*against*	22
convenir	*suit*	75
convertir	*convert*	97
corps	*body*	58
côte; sur la côte	*coast; coastal*	36
coton	*cotton*	13
couche-tard	*night owl*	10
coucher de soleil	*sunset*	93
couler	*flow*	78
couloir	*corridor*	34
coupe de cheveux	*haircut*	75
couramment	*fluently*	109
cours de chant	*vocal class*	20
coutumes	*customs*	36
couturier	*fashion designer*	75
couvert de nuages	*cloudy*	77
crème glacée	*ice cream*	60
crêpe	*pancake*	52
crier	*shout*	87
	yell	48
critiquer	*criticise / -ze*	22
croire	*believe*	56
croisière	*cruise*	32
croix	*cross*	107
croyance	*belief*	22
cru	*raw*	52
cuir	*leather*	75
cuivre	*brass*	79

D

de l'est	*eastern*	37
de partout	*from all over*	34
début	*beginning*	18
début des années …	*early …ies*	13
décontracté	*casual*	75
découverte	*discovery*	82
découvrir	*discover*	20
déçu	*disappointed*	20
dégoût	*disgust*	23
dehors	*outside*	46
déjà	*already*	30
démodé	*fashion (out of -)*	75
	old-fashioned	103
dépendre (de)	*depend (on)*	76
dépenses	*expenses*	79
dernier	*last*	37
dès	*as early as*	36
des milliers (de)	*thousands (of)*	93
dès que	*as soon as*	104
désespéré	*desperate*	64
détourné par des pirates	*hijacked*	27
détruire	*destroy*	27
deux tiers	*two thirds*	51
devenir	***become***	14
différent (de)	*different (from)*	34
diffuser (radio, TV)	***broadcast***	78
diminuer	*decrease*	84
disparu	*extinct*	47
disque	*record*	19
douane	*customs*	103
doubler (film)	*dub*	61
douceur	*softness*	61
douche	*shower*	58
douloureux	*painful*	34
doux	*soft*	61
	gentle	56
drapeau	*flag*	41
droit (n)	*right*	22
drôle	*fun*	48
du nord	*northern*	50
du sud	*southern*	13
dur	*hard*	20
durer	*last*	55

E

éclairage	*lighting*	79
éclairer	*light up*	50
écossais	*Scottish*	68
écouteurs	*earphones*	19
écran	*screen*	61
éducatif	*educational*	48
effacer	*erase*	57
effroyable	*frightful*	47
égal	*equal*	36
égoïste	*selfish*	25
élégant	*classy, stylish*	75
élever	***bring** up*	104
éliminer	*eliminate*	20
émeute	*riot*	97
émigrer	*emigrate*	51
émission	*programme*	20

Lexique

emmener	***take*** *(sbdy)*	56
empêcher de	*prevent (from+-ing)*	64
empreinte	*imprint*	64
empreinte de main	*handprint*	64
empreinte de pied	*footprint*	64
emprunter	*borrow*	70
en direct	*live* (adj)	20
en fait	*actually*	76
en forme	*fit*	20
en même temps	*at the same time*	16
en voie de disparition	*endangered*	47
encourager	*encourage*	22
endormi	*sleepy*	45
endroit	*place*	30
enlever	*remove*	57
ennui	*bore*	49
ennuyeux	*boring*	23
enregistrement	*recording*	19
enregistrer	*record* (v)	16
ensemble	*together*	44
ensuite	*afterwards*	44
entendre	***hear***	20
enterrement	*funeral*	81
enterrer	*bury*	79
entouré	*surrounded*	51
entraînement physique	*workout*	20
envahir	*invade*	62
envahisseur	*invader*	68
envoyer	***send***	18
épais	*thick*	61
épaisseur	*thickness*	61
éparpiller	*scatter*	48
épicé	*spicy*	32
épices	*spices*	79
éplucher	*peel*	95
éprouvant pour les nerfs	*nerve-racking*	21
épuisé	*exhausted*	87
érable	*maple tree*	42
escalade	*rock-climbing*	10
escalier	*stairs*	58
esclavage	*slavery*	13
esclave	*slave*	13
escroc	*crook*	56
espagnol	*Spanish*	37
espèce	*species*	47
espérance (de vie)	*expectancy (life -)*	92
espérer	*hope*	26
espoir	*hope* (n)	13
esprit ouvert	*open-minded*	103
essence	*petrol* (GB)	33
	gas (US)	33
essoufflé	***be*** *out of breath*	87
étage	*floor*	28
étaler	***spread***	60
état	*state*	13
éteindre un feu	***put*** *out a fire*	44
étonné	*puzzled*	59
étrange	*strange*	58
étranger (adj)	*foreign*	46
étranger (n)	*foreigner*	103
être allongé	***lie***	24
être égal	*not mind*	70
Ça m'est égal.	*I don't mind.*	
être en compétition	*compete*	78
être habillé	*dress* (v)	23
être humain	*human being*	23
études	*studies*	34
étudier	*study*	14
eux deux	*both of them*	15
événement	*event*	36
évoluer	*evolve*	13
excitant	*thrilling*	20
exemplaire	*copy*	19
exemple (par -)	*instance (for -)*	62
explorateur	*explorer*	42
exporter	*export*	43
expression	*phrase*	65
exprimer	*express*	13
extrêmement	*extremely*	23

F

façon	*way*	76
faible	*weak*	85
faim ; famine	*starvation*	97
faire confiance	*trust*	56
faire de la planche à voile	***go*** *windsurfing*	10
faire du canoë	*go canoeing*	44
faire du feu	*make a fire*	44
faire du ski nautique	***go*** *waterskiing*	10
faire du sport	***get*** *exercise*	50
faire du tourisme	***go*** *sightseeing*	47

faire la queue	*queue* (v)	77
faire semblant de	*pretend*	70
faire une randonnée	*hike*	30
faire une randonnée à dos de poney	***go** poney-trekking*	10
falaise	*cliff*	98
farine	*flour*	60
faune et flore	*wildlife*	47
faux, parodie de	*mock*	56
fermeture éclair	*zipper*	50
fermier	*farmer*	83
feu	*fire*	69
feu de brousse	*bushfire*	89
feuille	*leaf / leaves*	89
feux de circulation	*traffic light*	57
fidèle	*faithful*	79
film	*movie* (US);	61
	film (GB)	61
film à gros budget	*blockbuster*	61
film à suspense	*thriller*	58
film parlant	*talkie*	55
fin	*ending*	18
fin des années 60	*late sixties*	22
finir	*end up*	18
	finish	34
flèche	*arrow*	46
fonder	*found*	36
football	*soccer*	106
forêt tropicale	*rainforest*	89
formation	*training*	20
forme	*shape*	76
formé, qualifié	*trained*	104
fort	*strong*	20
fou	*crazy*	62
foudre	*lightning*	93
fourmi	*ant*	89
fourrure	*fur*	40
frapper	*knock*	56
frontière	*border*	68
fusil	*rifle*	46

G

gagnant	*winner*	65
gagner	***win***	20
gamin	*kid*	34
garde du corps	*bodyguard*	63
gaucher	*left-handed*	103
géant	*giant*	64
générique	*credits*	61
gentillesse	*kindness*	61
gilet de sauvetage	*life jacket*	44
grâce à	*thanks to*	20
graisse	*grease*	87
grand	*large* (city)	51
grandeur nature	*full-size*	65
grandir	***grow** up*	14
gratte-ciel	*skyscraper*	27
grec	*Greek*	37
griffe	*claw*	47
grimper	*climb up*	17
grossier	*crude*	23
grotte	*cave*	93
groupe de musique, orchestre	*band*	13
guêpe	*wasp*	89
guerre	*war*	27
Guerre de Sécession	*Civil War*	27

H

habillé; élégant	*formal*	75
habitant	*inhabitant*	28
habituellement	*usually*	21
hanté	*haunted*	59
harcèlement	*harassment*	103
haut	*top*	28
haut (son)	*loud*	19
hauteur	*height*	28
herbe	*grass*	89
hériter	*inherit*	107
hésiter	*hesitate*	34
heure de cours	*period* (GB)	108
histoire	*story*	23
histoires (faire des -)	*fuss (make a -)*	76
hit-parade	*charts*	23
hôte	*host*	70
hurler	*scream*	16

Lexique

I

image de synthèse	*computer-generated image*	60
immense	*huge*	51
immobile	*motionless*	48
imperméable (adj.)	*waterproof*	102
imposteur, faux	*fake*	56
impressionnant	*impressive*	93
improviser	*improvise*	55
inclure	*include*	13
informatique	*computer science*	34
ingénieur	*engineer*	104
inoffensif	*harmless*	91
inondé	*flooded*	86
instantané	*instant*	50
instrument de musique	*musical instrument*	14
interdire	*ban*	23
interdit	*forbidden*	97
introduire	*introduce*	22
irlandais	*Irish*	97
italien	*Italian*	37

J

jalousie	*jealousy*	20
japonais	*Japanese*	27
jeter	***throw***	79
jeux olympiques	*Olympic Games*	83
jouer; parier	*gamble*	30
journal intime	*diary*	48
journal populaire	*tabloid*	62
Juif	*Jew*	37
jusqu'à	*until*	37
juste	*right*	48

L

laine / en laine	*wool / woolen*	75
laisser tomber	*drop*	60
laisser, autoriser	***let***	44
langue	*language*	13
langue maternelle	*mother tongue*	35
lève-tôt	*early bird*	10
liberté	*freedom*	26
libre	*free*	83
lien	*tie*	69
lieu touristique	*tourist site*	51
logement	*accommodation*	103
loi	*law*	35
longueur	*length*	28
louer	*rent*	51
louer, embaucher	*hire*	58
lumière	*light*	46
lutte	*struggle*	22

M

magasin	*store*	51
maillot de bain	*bathing suit*	89
maïs	*corn* (US)	36
mal à la tête	*headache*	102
maladie	*disease*	36
malheureusement	*unfortunately*	20
mammifère	*mammal*	89
manifestation	*demonstration*	27
manipuler	*manipulate*	60
manquer	*miss*	20
Tu me manques	*I miss you*	
marche	*step*	28
mariage	*wedding*	81
marin	*sailor*	69
marionnette	*puppet*	60
marque	*brand name*	75
masque	*mask*	60
méchant	*nasty*	56
mélanger	*mix*	36
même	*even*	34
même si	*even though*	90
menacer	*threaten*	34
métro	*underground* (GB); *subway* (US)	33 33
metteur en scène	*director*	61
mettre en scène	*direct*	56
micro	*mike*	19
milliers (de)	*thousands (of)*	93
mince	*thin*	62
mode	*fashion*	76
mode de vie	*way of life*	22
moitié	*half (of)*	35
monde	*world*	34
moniteur	*instructor*	52

moniteur de colonie	*camp counsellor*	44
monnaie du pays	*currency*	41
montage (film)	*editing*	65
montagne	*mountain*	55
montant, quantité	*amount*	55
montrer	*show* (v)	23
morceau	*piece*	70
mort	*death*	58
mortel	*deadly*	91
mot	*word*	19
mouillé	*wet*	64
moulant	*tight-fitting*	75
mousson	*monsoon*	83
moustique	*mosquito*	89
mouton(s)	*sheep*	84
mouvement	*motion*	55
mur	*wall*	68
musée	*museum*	29
musée de peinture	*art gallery*	47
musicien	*musician*	13
musique classique	*classical music*	15
mystérieux	*mysterious*	58

N

nain	*dwarf*	65
naissance	*birth*	55
natal	*native*	13
navette spatiale	*space shuttle*	81
naviguer	*sail*	36
né	*born (**be**)*	14
ne pas respecter le règlement	***break** the rules*	34
ne pas s'occuper de	*ignore*	70
néerlandais	*Dutch*	82
neige	*snow*	60
nettoyer	*clean*	44
nez	*nose*	28
nid	*nest*	47
niveau	*level*	92
nord	*north*	27
nord (du)	*northern*	50
nous deux	*both of us*	15
nouveau	*newcomer*	103
nul	*naff*	75
nulle part	*not anywhere*	48

O

objets de valeur	*valuables*	67
occasion	*opportunity*	99
occasion (d' -)	*second-hand*	76
odeur	*smell*	95
or (en-)	*gold (golden)*	55
orchestre classique	*orchestra*	19
ordinateur	*computer*	55
oser	*dare*	70
ouragan	*hurricane*	56
ours	*bear*	49
ouverture	*opening*	83

P

pacifique	*peaceful*	97
pagayer	*paddle*	48
panneau publicitaire	*billboard*	57
panneau routier	*road sign*	107
panneau; signe	*sign*	34
par dessus tout	*above all*	22
pareil	*alike*	15
parmi	*among*	13
paroles de chanson	*lyrics*	19
particulièrement	*especially*	22
partie de (faire -)	*part (**be** part of)*	34
partout dans	*throughout*	23
partout où	*wherever*	106
pas du tout	*not at all*	20
pas encore	*not yet*	98
pas étonnant	*no wonder*	62
pas serré	*loose*	75
passé (dans le -)	*past (in the -)*	46
passer (temps)	***spend***	48
patinoire	*ice rink*	51
patron	*boss*	58
Pays-Bas (les -)	*Netherlands (the -)*	37
paysage	*landscape*	55
paysan	*peasant*	97
peau	*skin*	91
pêcher	*fish*	50
pendant	*during*	37
pendant que	*while*	13
pensionnaire	*boarder*	79
pensionnat	*boarding school*	89
perdre la face	***lose** face*	34
perdu de vue	*long-lost*	56

permis	*allowed*	13
permis de conduire	*driving licence*	89
permis de pêche	*fishing license*	105
permis de travail	*work permit*	103
personnage	*character*	55
personnel (n)	*staff*	104
peu de	*few*	83
peuplé	*populated*	35
phoque	*seal*	50
pièce de théâtre	*play* (n)	79
pire	*worse*	76
plage	*beach*	51
plateau de tournage	*set*	61
plein de	*loads of*	16
pleurer	*cry*	45
plongée (avec tuba)	*snorkelling*	10
plongeur	*diver*	88
plume	*feather*	47
plupart (la)	*most*	20
plus loin	*further*	92
plusieurs	*several*	20
poids	*weight*	28
poignarder	*stab*	58
poing	*fist*	64
pointu	*sharp*	53
pollué	*polluted*	49
portugais	*Portuguese*	82
pour toujours	*forever*	18
poursuivre	*follow around*	63
pourtant	*yet*	34
préféré	*favourite*	46
préférer	*would rather*	72
préjugé	*prejudice*	103
premièrement	*first*	34
prendre	***take***	56
près	*close*	63
présenter (qqn)	*introduce*	11
prêter	***lend***	25
principal de collège (GB)	*head teacher*	33
principalement	*mainly; mostly*	37
prise de vue	*shot*	61
prise électrique	*plug*	102
privé	*private*	62
privilégié	*exclusive*	62
prix	*price*	28
prix Nobel	*Nobel Prize*	107
problème	*trouble*	13
producteur	*producer*	55
produire	*produce*	55
projecteur	*spotlight*	17
projeter de	*plan* (v)	32
propriétaire	*owner*	92
protégé	*protected*	49
protestation	*protest*	22
public	*audience*	16
publicité	*advertisement*	64
	commercial (TV, radio)	66
puce	*flea*	76
puissance	*power*	69
purée de pommes de terre	*mashed potatoes*	60

Q

quartier	*borough* (New York)	28
quelques	*few (a -)*	21
queue	*tail*	47
qui donne la chair de poule	*spooky*	59
qui s'ennuie de chez lui	*homesick*	20
quiconque	*whoever*	74
quitter	***leave***	18
quotidien	*daily*	64

R

raison	*reason*	37
ramasser	*collect*	86
cueillir	*pick*	13
ramer	*row*	72
rassembler	*gather*	88
réagir	*react*	23
recette	*recipe*	70
réchauffement de la planète	*global warming*	85
recherche	*research*	100
reconnaître	*recognise / -ze*	58
refléter	*reflect*	22
refrain	*chorus*	19
réfugié	*refugee*	37
regarder fixement	*stare*	48
région	*area*	40
règlement	*rule*	34

règne	*reign*	69
regretter	*regret* (v)	20
rejeter	*reject*	22
rejoindre	*join*	41
relier	*link*	37
religieux	*religious*	36
remarquer	*notice*	76
rempli de monde	*crowded*	29
renommée	*fame*	62
renvoi	*suspension*	34
répétition	*rehearsal*	20
réprimer	*crush*	97
repu, rassasié	*full*	70
requin	*shark*	89
ressembler à	*look like*	60
	sound like	60
rester	*remain*	97
	stay	20
réussir	*succeed*	34
révéler	*reveal*	58
revenir de loin	***come** a long way*	34
réserve	*reservation*	36
revolver	*gun*	35
rire (n)	*laugh*	45
rive	*bank* (river)	79
Rocheuses (les -)	*Rockies (the -)*	30
rôle	*part*	61
	role	58
rôle principal	*leading role*	58
roman	*novel*	52
ronchonner	*moan*	70
rouge vif	*bright red*	50
rouillé	*rusty*	104
ruban	*ribbon*	106
rude	*harsh*	51
Ruée vers l'Or	*Gold Rush*	37
russe	*Russian*	37
rythme	*beat; rhythm*	19

S

sable	*sand*	49
s'adapter /adapter	*adapt*	21
saigner	***bleed***	95
sang	*blood*	60
sans	*without*	51
sans abri	*homeless*	47
santé	*health*	92
s'approcher de	***get** close (to)*	63
s'attendre à	*expect*	20
sauf	*except*	36
sauf si	*unless*	104
saumon	*salmon*	99
sauvage	*wild*	44
scène	*stage*	16
se battre	***fight***	22
se calmer	*simmer (down)*	48
se cogner contre	*bump (into ...)*	34
se débrouiller avec	*cope with*	62
se débarasser de	***get** rid of*	58
se demander	*wonder*	71
se déplacer	***get** around*	51
se disputer	*argue*	18
se faire traiter de tous les noms	***be** called names*	62
se lever (soleil)	***rise***	10
se nourrir (de)	*feed (on)*	50
se passer	*happen*	16
se plaindre	*complain*	70
se protéger	***take** cover*	48
se rebeller	*rebel*	23
se rendre à, aller à	***get** (to)*	28
se sentir	***feel***	20
se terminer	***come** to an end*	55
séance	*session*	20
s'échapper	*escape*	51
sécheresse	*drought*	89
s'écraser	*crash*	27
secteur	*district*	22
sel	*salt*	49
selon	*according to*	65
sembler	*seem*	48
s'ennuyer	***get** bored with*	18
s'entendre	***get** on*	18
sentiment	*feeling*	13
se présenter	*introduce*	11
serpent	*snake*	90
serpent à sonnette	*rattlesnake*	30
serré	*tight*	75
s'éteindre	***go** out* (light)	17
seuil de pauvreté	*poverty level*	35
seul	*alone*	44
s'évanouir	*faint*	17
sévère	*strict*	20
s'excuser	*apologize*	70
siège arrière	*back seat*	48
s'installer	*settle*	37

sirop	*syrup*	60
situer	*locate*	34
société d'informatique	*dot.com company*	100
soie	*silk*	75
sol	*soil*	49
soldat	*soldier*	82
solitude	*loneliness*	13
sombre	*dark*	56
son	*sound* (n)	13
sorte	*kind* (n)	13
souffler	***blow***	56
souffrir de	*suffer from*	23
soupçonner	*suspect*	58
sourire	*smile*	18
sous-titre	*subtitle*	61
soutenir	*support*	20
souterrain	*underground*	49
spectacle	*show*	20
station (touristique)	*resort*	47
stimuler	*boost*	51
succès (qui a du -)	*successful*	47
sud / du sud	*South / southern*	13
supplémentaire	*extra*	61
supporter	***put** up with*	48
sur la côte	*coastal*	85
surnom	*nickname*	65
survivre	*survive*	36
sympathique	*friendly*	70

T

tabac	*tobacco*	36
tableau (peinture)	*painting*	79
tache	*stain*	87
taille	*size*	75
talent	*talent*	20
tambour	*drum*	13
tard	*late*	10
taux	*rate*	92
taxi	*cab* (US)	29
tel que, comme	*such as*	13
télé/spectateur	*viewer*	20
télécommandé	*radio-controlled*	60
tenir (un commerce)	***run***	104
tentative	*attempt*	97
terre	*land*	36
terrifié	*terrified*	59
théâtre	*drama*	67
toboggan	*slide*	51
toit	*roof*	79
tomber en panne	***break** down*	17
tôt	*early*	48
toucher	*touch*	34
tournage (film)	*shooting*	62
tournant, virage	*bend*	48
tournant	*turning point*	58
tournée (faire une -)	*tour (**go** on -)*	20
tourner un film	***shoot***	55
tout	*everything*	48
toute la journée	*all day long*	48
toute l'année	*all year round*	50
traîneau à chiens	*dogsled*	46
tranquillement	*quietly*	24
transpirer	*sweat* (v)	20
trembler	*tremble*	20
trésor	*treasure*	56
tribu	*tribe*	36
tribunal	*court*	62
triste	*sad*	18
troisièmement	*thirdly*	34
tronc	*trunk*	89
trottoir	*sidewalk* (US); *pavement* (GB)	33 33
typhon	*typhoon*	89

U

utile	*useful*	52
utiliser	*use*	13

V

vacances	*vacation* (US)	32
vague	*wave*	37
vaincre	*defeat*	27
vénéneux	*poisonous*	90
vent	*wind*	29
ventilateur	*fan*	58
verglacé	*icy*	49
vérifier	*check*	64
verre	*glass*	51
vers	*towards*	57

Y

Références des textes

p. 48 :

Wow Canada!, © Vivien Bowers 1999,
Greey de Pencier Books Inc.

p. 113 :

Sunday Bloody Sunday, Words and Music by U2,
© Blue Mountain Music Ltd.
Used by permission of Music Sales Ltd.

pp. 118 à 123 :

Frankenstein, retold by Patrick Nobes,
Collection Oxford Bookworms,
Oxford University Press

pp. 124 à 127 :

Not dressed like that, you don't!
The diaries of a teenager… and her mother…
© Yvonne Coppard 1991,
Piccadilly Press Ltd

Symboles phonétiques

Les sons voyelles

[iː] teacher	[ɪ] film	[eɪ] name	[aɪ] time	[ɔɪ] boy
[ɔː] ball	[ɒ] rock			
[uː] school	[ʊ] look	[əʊ] home	[aʊ] now	
[ɑː] class	[æ] cat			
[ɜː] girl	[e] test			
[ʌ] lunch				
[ə] across	[ɪə] here	[ʊə] sure	[eə] chair	

Les consonnes autres que p, b, t, d, f, v, s, z, m, n, l ,r

[k] car	[w] want	[kw] quick	[θ] three	[ð] this	[ŋ] sing
[ʃ] English	[tʃ] chair	[ʒ] usual	[dʒ] jazz	[j] yes	[h] hair

L'accent de mot

accent principal :	[ˈ]	America	[əˈmerɪkə]
accent secondaire :	[ˌ]	nationality	[ˌnæʃəˈnælətɪ]

Verbes irréguliers

Base verbale	Prétérit	Participe passé	Traduction
B			
be	was, were	been	*être*
bear [eə]	bore	born, borne	*porter, supporter* (born : *né*)
beat [iː]	beat	beaten	*battre*
become	became [eɪ]	become	*devenir*
begin	began	begun	*commencer*
bite [aɪ]	bit	bitten [ɪ]	*mordre*
bleed [iː]	bled	bled	*saigner*
blow [əʊ]	blew [uː]	blown [əʊ]	*souffler*
break [eɪ]	broke [əʊ]	broken [əʊ]	*casser*
bring	brought [ɔː]	brought [ɔː]	*apporter*
broadcast	broadcast	broadcast	*diffuser, émettre*
build [ɪ]	built [ɪ]	built [ɪ]	*construire*
burn [ɜː]	burnt [ɜː]	burnt [ɜː]	*brûler*
buy [aɪ]	bought [ɔː]	bought [ɔː]	*acheter*
C			
catch	caught [ɔː]	caught [ɔː]	*attraper*
choose [uː]	chose [əʊ]	chosen [əʊ]	*choisir*
come	came [eɪ]	come	*venir*
cost	cost	cost	*coûter*
cut	cut	cut	*couper*
D			
do	did	done	*faire*
draw [ɔː]	drew [uː]	drawn [ɔː]	*tirer, dessiner*
dream [iː]	dreamt [e]	dreamt [e]	*rêver*
drink	drank	drunk	*boire*
drive [aɪ]	drove	driven [ɪ]	*conduire*
E			
eat [ɪː]	ate [e]	eaten [ɪː]	*manger*
F			
fall [ɔː]	fell	fallen [ɔː]	*tomber*
feed	fed	fed	*nourrir*
feel	felt	felt	*sentir, ressentir*
fight [aɪ]	fought [ɔː]	fought [ɔː]	*combattre, se battre*
find [aɪ]	found [aʊ]	found [aʊ]	*trouver*
fly [aɪ]	flew [uː]	flown [əʊ]	*voler (dans l'air)*
forbid	forbade [æ]	forbidden	*interdire*
forget	forgot	forgotten	*oublier*
forgive	forgave [eɪ]	forgiven	*pardonner*
freeze	froze [əʊ]	frozen [əʊ]	*geler*
G			
get	got	got	*obtenir, devenir*
give	gave [eɪ]	given	*donner*
go	went	gone [ɒ]	*aller*
grow [əʊ]	grew [uː]	grown [əʊ]	*grandir, faire pousser*
H			
hang	hung	hung	*accrocher*
have	had	had	*avoir*
hear [ɪə]	heard [ɜː]	heard [ɜː]	*entendre*
hide [aɪ]	hid	hidden [ɪ]	*(se) cacher*
hit	hit	hit	*frapper*
hold	held	held	*tenir*
hurt	hurt	hurt	*faire mal, blesser*
K			
keep	kept	kept	*garder*
know	knew [juː]	known [əʊ]	*savoir, connaître*

Base verbale	Prétérit	Participe passé	Traduction
		L	
lay [eɪ]	laid [eɪ]	laid [eɪ]	*poser (à plat)*
lead [iː]	led	led	*mener*
learn [ɜː]	learnt [ɜː]	learnt [ɜː]	*apprendre*
leave [iː]	left	left	*quitter, partir*
lend	lent	lent	*prêter*
let	let	let	*laisser, permettre*
lie [aɪ]	lay [eɪ]	lain [eɪ]	*être allongé*
light [aɪ]	lit	lit	*allumer, éclairer*
lose [uː]	lost [ɒ]	lost [ɒ]	*perdre*
		M	
make	made [eɪ]	made [eɪ]	*faire, fabriquer*
mean [iː]	meant [e]	meant [e]	*signifier, vouloir dire*
meet	met	met	*rencontrer*
		P	
pay	paid [eɪ]	paid [eɪ]	*payer*
put	put	put	*poser, mettre*
		R	
read [iː]	read [e]	read [e]	*lire*
ride [aɪ]	rode	ridden [ɪ]	*faire du cheval*
ring	rang	rung	*sonner*
rise [aɪ]	rose	risen [ɪ]	*s'élever; se lever (soleil)*
run	ran	run	*courir*
		S	
say	said [e]	said [e]	*dire*
see	saw [ɔː]	seen	*voir*
sell	sold	sold	*vendre*
send	sent	sent	*envoyer*
set	set	set	*poser, fixer, mettre*
shake [eɪ]	shook	shaken [eɪ]	*secouer*

Base verbale	Prétérit	Participe passé	Traduction
shine [aɪ]	shone [ɒ]	shone [ɒ]	*briller*
shoot [uː]	shot	shot	*tirer (arme à feu)*
show	showed	shown	*montrer*
shut	shut	shut	*fermer*
sing	sang	sung	*chanter*
sit	sat	sat	*être assis*
sleep	slept	slept	*dormir*
smell	smelt	smelt	*sentir (odeur)*
speak	spoke	spoken	*parler*
spell	spelt	spelt	*épeler*
spend	spent	spent	*passer (temps); dépenser*
spoil	spoilt	spoilt	*gâter*
spread [e]	spread [e]	spread [e]	*étaler*
stand	stood	stood	*être debout*
steal [iː]	stole [əʊ]	stolen	*voler (dérober)*
stick	stuck	stuck	*coller*
sweep	swept	swept	*balayer*
swim	swam	swum	*nager*
		T	
take	took	taken	*prendre*
teach [iː]	taught [ɔː]	taught [ɔː]	*enseigner*
tear [eə]	tore [ɔː]	torn [ɔː]	*déchirer*
tell	told	told	*dire, raconter*
think	thought [ɔː]	thought [ɔː]	*penser*
throw [əʊ]	threw [uː]	thrown [əʊ]	*jeter*
		U	
understand	understood	understood	*comprendre*
		W	
wake (up) [eɪ]	woke (up) [əʊ]	woken (up) [əʊ]	*(se) réveiller*
wear [eə]	wore [ɔː]	worn [ɔː]	*porter (vêtement)*
win	won [ʌ]	won [ʌ]	*gagner*
write [aɪ]	wrote [əʊ]	written [ɪ]	*écrire*

Attention

1. Orthographe voisine

feel	felt	felt	*(se) sentir*
fall	fell	fallen	*tomber*
lie	lay	lain	*être allongé*
lie (*régulier*)	lied	lied	*mentir*
lay	laid	laid	*poser (à plat)* (lay the table: *mettre le couvert*)

2. oo / o

ch**oo**se	ch**o**se [əʊ]	ch**o**sen [əʊ]	*choisir*
l**o**se [uː]	l**o**st [ɒ]	l**o**st [ɒ]	*perdre*

3. ought / aught: [ɔːt]

bring	br**ou**ght	br**ou**ght	*apporter*
buy	b**ou**ght	b**ou**ght	*acheter*
fight	f**ou**ght	f**ou**ght	*combattre, se battre*
catch	c**au**ght	c**au**ght	*attraper*
teach	t**au**ght	t**au**ght	*enseigner*

4. Une consonne / deux consonnes

forbid	forbade	forbi**dd**en	*interdire*
hide	hid	hi**dd**en	*(se) cacher*
ride	rode	ri**dd**en	*faire du cheval*
bite	bit	bi**tt**en	*mordre*
forget	forgot	forgo**tt**en	*oublier*
write	wrote	wri**tt**en	*écrire*

Table des illustrations

10-g ph © Mike Yamashita / Rapho
10-m ph © Rapho
10-d ph © Karnow /Cosmos
12 ph © Corbis
12-h ph © Philippe Halsman / Magnum Photos
12-bg ph © Micelotta / Image Direct / Sipa
13-h ph © Lola / Dalle
13-m ph © D. Miller / Woodfin Camp / Cosmos
13-b ph © Rob Crandall / Cosmos
14-h ph © SNAP / Cosmos
14-bg ph © Bob Gruen / Stills
14-bd ph © Van Houten / Dalle
15-hg ph © RM / Corbis
15-hd ph © Veuige / Dalle
19 ph © Tina Korhonen / Rep Folo / Dalle
20 ph © Cheung Wattie / Camera Press / Gamma
21-g ph © Cheung Wattie / Camera Press / Gamma
21-d ph © Marshall Joyce / Gamma
22-h ph © Time Pix / Cosmos
22-b ph © Benoit Decout / Réa
23-h ph © Homer Sykes 1982 Woodfin Camp & Associates / Cosmos
23-b ph © Claude Gassian
26 ph © S.Fautre/Ask Images
28-m ph © Yann Arthus Bertrand / Altitude
28-bg ph © Stefano Amantini / Ask Images
28-bd ph © Yann Arthus Bertrand/Altitude
30-h ph © S.Grandadam / Hoa Qui
30-m ph © Bruno Pérousse / Hoa Qui
30-b ph © F.Gohier / Hoa Qui
31 ph © Stéphane Frances / Hémisphères
32-h ph © G.Bras / Rapho
32-mh ph © Frilet / Sipa
32-mb ph © J.B.Rabouan / P.Fiori / Hémisphères.
32-b ph © Patrick Frilet / Hémisphères
34 ph © Roswell Angier / Picture Group / Rapho
35-hg ph © Bertrand Rieger / Hémisphères
35-hd ph © P.Horre / ANA
36-h ph © Sally Fear / Impact Photos / Cosmos
36-m ph © Norman Rockwell
36-b ph © Tallandier
37-h ph © Rue des Archives
37-m ph © John Elk III / Cosmos
37-b ph © Martha Cooper / Ask Images
40 ph © Richard T.Nowitz / Corbis
42-hd ph © Philippe Renault
42-bg ph © Jacques Ducoin / ANA
42-mh ph © Galen Rowell / Corbis
42-mm ph © DR
42-md ph © Philippe Renault
42-bg ph © Jacques Ducoin/ANA
42-bd ph © Mc Hugh T. / Jacana
44 ph © K. Straiton / Hoa-qui
46-g ph © Alexander / Cosmos
46-d ph © Alexander / Cosmos
48/49 ph © Christian Heeb / Hémisphères
48-h ph © Frédéric / Jacana
48-b ph © Tom Walker / Jacana
49 ph © Manaud / Icone / Hoa-qui
50-h ph © Pekka Parvainen / SPL / Cosmos
50-m ph © Bourseiller / Hoa-qui
50-b ph © UWE WALZ / Jacana
51-h ph © CNTower Canada's Wonder of the World
51-m ph © Xavier Testelin / Rapho
51-b ph © Luis Ortéo / Hémisphères
54/55 ph © Kobal collection
54-g ph © Collection D. Bouteiller
54-d ph © Archives Hatier
55-g ph © Cat's collection
55-d ph © Kobal collection
58-h ph © Archives Hatier
58-m ph © Archives Hatier
58-b ph © Collection D. Bouteiller
59-hg ph © Photos12.com - Collection cinéma
59-hd ph © Archives Hatier
59-mg ph © Photos12.com-Collection cinéma
59-md ph © Collection D. Bouteiller
60 ph © Men in Black II TM © Columbia Pictures Industries, Inc. All Rights Reserved
61 ph © Adam Woolfitt / Corbis
62-h ph © Collection D. Bouteiller
62-b ph © Photos12.com-Collection cinéma
63-g ph © Laurence Schwartzwold / Corbis Sygma
63-d ph © Kim Kulish / Corbis Sygma
64-h ph © Photos12.com-Collection cinéma
64-m ph © Albert Ortega / Sipa

Table des illustrations *(suite)*

64-b	ph © Photos12.com-Collection cinéma
65-g	ph © T. O'Neill / Woodfin Camp / Cosmos
65-h	ph © Kevork Djansezian / AP / Sipa
65-d	ph © Photos12.com-Collection cinéma
68/69	ph © Alex Eon-Duval / Ask Images
72-hg	ph © John Walmsley
72-hd	ph © Coulson Jez Insight / Turner Neil / Réa
72-mg	ph © Jonathan Olley / Network
72-md	ph © Claudie / Sunset
72 bg	ph © Horst &Daniel Zielke/ Laif / Rea
72-bd	ph © J. P. Sharpe / Sunset
73-g	ph © Alex Eon-Duval / Ask Images
73-d	ph © John Walmsley
74-hg	ph © Marco / Ask Images
74-hd	ph © Spectrum / Sunset
74-mg	ph © Corbis
74-md	ph © Benoit Decout / Réa
76-h	ph © Gideon Mendel / Network / Rapho
76-b	ph © S. Cagnoni / Report Digital / Réa
77-g	ph © Ariel Skelley / Corbis
77-d	ph © Dylan Martinez / Corbis Sygma
78-h	ph © François Le Diascorn / Top
78-b	ph © Zefa-Palmer / Kane / Hoa-qui
79-h	ph © Gideon Mendel / Network / Rapho
79-m	ph © Steve Lemere / Sipa
79-b	ph © Spectrum / Sunset
82	ph © Gérard Lacz / Sunset
84-mg	ph © Georg Gerster / Rapho
84-md	ph © Matthieu Colin / Hémisphères
84-bg	ph © Marco Polo
84-bd	ph © Panos / Editing
85-h	ph © Serge Attal / Ask Images
85-m	ph © Gabriel Bouys / AFP
88-h	ph © D.Hancock / Cosmos
88-g	ph © S.Fautre / Ask Images
88-mh	ph © Pierre Boulat / Cosmos
88-mm	ph © Hervé Hughes
88-mb	ph © Serge Attal / Ask Images
88-b	ph © Animals Animals / Sunset
89	ph © Hervé Hughes / Hémisphères
90/91	ph © Spectrum / Sunset
90-g	ph © Patrick Frilet / Hémisphères
91-d	ph © F. Le Diascorn / Rapho
92/93	ph © I. Bandy / Top
92-h	ph © Bettmann / Corbis
92-b	ph © Rick Smolan / Cosmos
93-h	ph © Gérard Sioen / Rapho
93-b	ph © Karnow / Cosmos
96-h	ph © Silvester / Rapho
96-m	ph © Claude Thibault / Ask Images
96-b	ph © Claude Thibault / Ask Images
97	ph © Claude Thibault / Ask Images
98-hg	ph © Nutan / Rapho
98-hd	ph © Claudie / Sunset
98-mg	ph © Nutan / Rapho
98-mm	ph © Hervé Champollion / Top
98-md	ph © Nutan / Rapho
98-bg	ph © Guy Christian / Hémisphères
98-bd	ph © Claude Thibault / Ask Images
103	ph © D.R.
104	ph © Philippe Sohiez
105	ph © Bruno Perousse / Hoa-Qui
106-h	ph © C.Ires / Explorer
106-m	ph © Matthieu Colin / Hémisphères
106-b	ph © Vandystadt
107-h	ph © The Bridgeman Art Library
107-mg	ph © Penguin Books Ltd 2000
107-md	ph © The Public Trustee as Executor of the Estate of George Bernard Shaw, 1957
107-b	ph © Georg Gerster / Rapho
110	ph © Joseph Martin / AKG, Paris
112	ph © Bettmann/Corbis
115	ph © Bridgeman
131	ph © AKG, Paris
134	ph © Robert & Collins Senior Dictionnaires Le Robert 2002

Malgré nos efforts, il nous a été impossible de joindre certains photographes ou leurs ayant-droits ainsi que les éditeurs ou les ayant-droits de certains textes pour solliciter l'autorisation de reproduction, mais nous avons réservé en notre comptabilité tous les droits usuels.

Iconographie : Service Illustration

Imprimé en Italie par Grafica Editoriale Printing, Bologne

Dépôt légal N° 32918 - Juillet 2006

The English-speaking world